SHORT STORIES FOR SENIORS

51 Heartwarming Stories for Stimulating Memory, Cognition, and Relieving Stress

PHILLIP WILLIS

TABLE OF CONTENTS

INTRODUCTION

Everyone has a story, one worth remembering and recounting to others. Sometimes we only become aware of how poignant and influential particular moments in our lives have been long after they have passed.

This book contains 51 heartwarming and endearing short stories to take you on the most important journey of all. You can enjoy these stories from the coziest, comfiest sofa in your home and with the company of someone willing to hold your hand and listen, or perhaps read these stories to you. With so many amazing tales inside these pages, your still-vibrant heartstrings are sure to be pulled as you read or hear about moments in the lives of others that will rekindle the spark of moments that have passed but are still very much alive in your consciousness.

CHAPTER 1

FIVE STORIES ABOUT FAMILY

DURNWIN

David had never seen the toy store so busy. Several young children, all about the same age as him, were running around admiring their favorite toys. Some children quickly grabbed the plastic boxes they wanted, whether they contained an action figure or perhaps a dinosaur figurine, and handed the box over to their parents as they pleaded for what they enthusiastically explained was a very necessary purchase.

The crowded, congested feeling was only pronounced by the small size of the store.

However, David knew exactly where he needed to go.

Still holding his father's hand, David pulled him through the narrow aisles, dodging other families until they got to where they needed to be: right in front of Durnwin.

"Here it is, Dad!" David exclaimed as he pointed his small index finger at the plastic, medieval-looking sword resting inside a box almost the same size as David himself.

John, David's father, put one hand on his tie as he leaned over to survey the sword before ultimately looking at the price.

"That's quite expensive for a toy…" he said.

This statement was of no consequence to young David, who was practically vibrating with excitement. He explained to his father that it was a magic sword like the one in the movies he watched at home, but that didn't excite his father quite as much as David had hoped.

"I'll make you a deal," John began as he stood up straight and looked at David stoically. "When you manage to ride your bike across the grass field outside our house, I will give you the money to buy the sword."

David's expression turned grave with disappointment.

"But it's the last one they have! Someone else might take it!" he whined.

"You said you're tired of being the only one of your friends who can't ride a bike, so this should be as important to you as it is to me," said his father.

David regretted having expressed his frustrations about not knowing how to ride a bike and not practicing like he had promised his father.

After a brief but fervent protest, David acquiesced to his father's terms and ambled back to the car with a look of utter defeat.

Once they got home, it seemed later than it was due to the rain clouds forming in the sky. However, David's worry that another lucky child (with perhaps a more reasonable father) would buy the sword was so intense that he got his bike and headed to the grass field opposite his house.

"David, it's going to rain; let's practice tomorrow!" John exclaimed, but David insisted.

Once both father and son made it to the field, they noticed it was muddier than usual.

"I don't have the right shoes for this, David. Let me go home and change. They're going to get muddy, and this is what I wear to the office."

"NO!" David exclaimed as he pulled his bike onto the far end of the field.

Visibly frustrated, John accompanied his son—dirtying his leather shoes in the process—to where David would begin biking.

The air was cold, and the clouds were beginning to make threatening sounds, but David was unfazed by the approaching tempest.

At first, the mud made it nearly impossible for David to find his balance—let alone move the bike forward.

John kept bending down to help David back up, but David pulled away from his father angrily. He was still indignant over not owning Durnwin, the magic sword.

After several minutes, rain began to fall, but John said nothing; he knew his son was determined to ride his bike to the end of the grass field.

"You can do it; I believe in you!" yelled John.

David looked at the gray sky and felt the cold droplets hit his nose and cheeks.

This time, he leaped onto the bike and rode it flawlessly across the entire field. When he got off and turned to see if his father had been watching, John was already running towards him with arms wide open.

David and John hugged jubilantly. They were oblivious to the pouring rain soaking both of them.

***

The next afternoon, John was in a particularly dreadful mood when he returned from work. However, he was looking forward to seeing David brandishing Durnwin, which he had surely purchased with his mother while John was at the office.

John went into his son's room and asked him about the sword.

David smiled and ran to his closet, where he pulled out a cardboard shoebox and handed it to his dad.

John was confused, since the box would have had to be about three times that size to contain the sword. After noticing the look of utter joy in his son's eyes, John opened the box and saw a pair of new leather shoes resting inside.

"I chose to buy these for you instead. Thank you for helping me learn to ride a bike," David exclaimed gleefully.

The Kitten

"You're wrong!" Tom protested as he sat in the backseat of his parents' car, cradling the small kitten in his arms.

"Buddy is a very energetic dog, and you know it's not safe for the kitten to be around him," Tom's mother reasoned as she drove toward the nearby forest, where she had instructed her son to drop off the young stray that kept venturing into their home.

"We've had Buddy for two years, and he's never hurt another dog. How can you think he would hurt a kitten?!" argued Tom.

"We literally saw him with his mouth over her little head!"

"He was just playing!" Tom exclaimed.

The argument continued for the entire drive. Tom's mother was not an animal person. Finally convincing her to allow Tom to have Buddy, their playful golden retriever, had been a long and arduous effort, but Tom finally had the dog he had always dreamed of.

For the past week, a tiny gray kitten who couldn't have been more than a year old kept venturing into their front yard, which Buddy frequented. Tom reveled with joy every time he saw the kitten. His mother, on the other hand, did not.

Tom ignored the sound of twigs and leaves under the tires as they reached the forest; his gaze was on the kitten, which he did not want to relinquish to the woods. He sat silently stroking the kitten, which he hadn't even named yet, until his mother exited the car and opened the passenger seat.

A part of Tom wondered if his mother was right: if Buddy would one day hurt the kitten—by accident, of course. After all, Buddy was still very young, and he shared Tom's zest for adventure, which sometimes led to the occasional mishap.

Once Tom and his mother were deep inside the forest, Tom knelt and gently put the kitten down. Before he could say goodbye to the kitten, it had already darted behind the trees, quickly moving out of sight.

The ride back home was the opposite of the ride to the woods. Tom was utterly silent, looking out the window and hoping to see the kitten again.

"STOP!" Tom suddenly exclaimed, which made his mother jolt and swerve the car.

"What is it?!" she gasped.

"There are dogs! Big angry dogs!"

"What?!" Tom's mother asked as she stopped the car and looked at her son, her face turning red.

Tom explained that he had seen two very intimidating-looking dogs running toward the spot where they had dropped off the kitten and that they needed to go back to rescue her.

Before his mother could finish explaining why that wasn't going to happen, Tom opened the door and ran back to where he'd released the kitten, ignoring his mother's screams for him to come back.

Once he made it to where they'd left the kitten, he called out to the young feline desperately. He had only been looking around for a few minutes before his mother ran over to him and forcibly pulled him back to the car.

"Do you want those dogs to hurt you?!" she exclaimed as she slammed the door shut, walked over to the driver's side, and slid in.

She was right. Tom hadn't considered the danger of calling out in the middle of the woods and potentially attracting the attention of the large dogs he'd seen earlier.

Once Tom and his mother got home, Tom refused to exit the car.

"I was worried about you. I didn't want you to get hurt, Tom. I'm sorry," she apologized.

"I don't want the kitten to get hurt, but maybe it's too late."

Without saying anything, Tom's mother made her way to the backseat and sat by her son's side, putting her arm around him and stroking his hair. They stayed this way for a long time before they decided to go inside for a snack.

Tom entered the house and saw something in the front yard through the sliding glass door. He darted toward it and slid it open.

"Mom, look!"

Tom's mother came running and put her hand over her mouth when she saw what Tom was pointing at.

The kitten was fast asleep on Buddy's fluffy stomach, its little head gently moving up and down as Buddy breathed in and out.

Buddy opened his eyes and looked at Tom, his mother, and finally at the kitten sleeping on his belly before closing them again and going back to sleep.

Tom knelt and began stroking them both. He looked up at his mother, who was smiling at the sight in front of her. Without saying anything, Tom knew from his mother's satisfied expression that he and Buddy now had a new, lifelong friend.

THE BOX HOUSE

Albert parked in front of his house and stayed inside the car for a long, contemplative moment as he looked at the small, white house he would maybe never see again. He had built this house, just like he'd built many others—some even currently inhabited by his nephews or friends.

It always brought Albert great joy remembering that he had built the houses that were giving shelter and keeping many of his loved ones warm. However, now that he was due to move to the big city to join a multinational architecture firm, he felt his heart twinge with sadness over the loss of the first home he had ever built: his own.

Once inside, Albert was greeted enthusiastically by his daughter Ella, whose blonde pigtails bounced as she ran to greet him in her little pink Minnie Mouse dress.

"Do we get to stay?" Ella demanded with a smile so bright and intoxicating that it seemed as if she was confident the answer would be the one she was hoping for.

After yet another moment of hesitation, Albert sheepishly shook his head in denial.

Ella's green eyes filled with tears upon hearing this devastating news. However, she did not protest like she had the previous days. Instead, Ella bowed her head in sullen acquiescence and disappeared, probably into her room.

Albert called to her, but she ignored him, which bothered Albert much more than her vehement demands that they stay. Ella had always relished the fact that she lived in the very first house her father had built—so much so that she constantly announced to everyone that one day she would grow up to be an architect like her father and that she would build a house just for the two of them.

Albert became tormented by the worry that perhaps this move would make Ella lose sight of those childish, yet poignant and heartfelt aspirations.

***

A couple of days later, on a particularly wet and downcast Saturday morning, Albert ensconced himself in his bedroom. He was surrounded by so many cardboard boxes that it was impossible to see what the actual floor of the bedroom looked like anymore.

He had initially requested Ella's help with packing, but given the way she had been willfully ignoring him for the past couple of days, he had rescinded his invitation to make packing a family affair.

The door to his bedroom opened and Ella walked in. Her hair was down, and she had a determined look on her face. She made her way through the spacious bedroom and gathered up as many cardboard boxes as she could carry with her little hands before disappearing through the open door.

Albert surmised that she must be worried that her things would be left behind unless she helped pack, which made him smile. He wondered whether he should try and help her, but ultimately decided to let her have her space.

After a couple of hours of packing, the white carpet was once again visible. There were cardboard boxes everywhere, making Albert feel more melancholy than he had expected. He felt the urge to grab a box cutter and free his belongings, but he knew that he had to be strong, especially in front of Ella.

As Albert slowly made his way to Ella's bedroom, he pondered how to make her understand that all of this was happening because he wanted to keep building houses for other people and that he was sorry for breaking the promise he'd made many years ago that they would never leave their home. As much as he tried to think of the right thing to say, he realized that words could not explain his sorrow.

Before Albert could open the door, it swung open by itself, which frightened him.

"Are you ready?" Ella asked, her eyes once more glimmering with joy.

"For what?"

"Come inside!" Ella replied as she pulled her father into the bedroom.

Once inside, Albert noticed about six cardboard boxes taped together to form what seemed like a makeshift castle. There were flowers, vines, and windows drawn on the first four boxes, which were stacked on top of each other, and the two boxes on each side had a fence drawn on them.

"What is this?" he asked.

"This is the house I built for us. We can take it with us and live in it wherever we are in the world!" Ella rejoiced.

Albert smiled and followed his daughter. He sat down in the space she'd built inside the first four boxes and looked at all the drawings of kitchen utensils and bookshelves she'd made.

"It's perfect. We'll take it with us wherever we go," Albert said as a tear ran down his cheek.

MAGIC MOUNTAIN

Maggie repeatedly nodded as she listened to Matthew, her six-year-old son, continuously explain how amazing Magic Mountain was. Initially, she thought Matthew was referring to the amusement park ride, which made it very confusing when she heard that the teacher had read a book about it to the entire class at school.

"No!" Matthew protested, "Magic Mountain is a place with a secret castle that only appears for children who are ready to become king and rule Magic Mountain forever!"

Maggie smiled as she listened to Matthew's excitement about the stories he heard in school. Matthew had always had a vibrant imagination that took him places she could not always follow. As she drove to their favorite restaurant, she wondered if the baby currently growing inside her would have an imagination that was just as active; after all, it was going to be another boy.

"And what does the king have to do in his kingdom?" Maggie asked as she parked the car on the gravel road leading up to the steakhouse.

"He protects the castle from dragons and teaches his knights how to fight and be brave!" Matthew proclaimed.

"That's an enormous responsibility!" Maggie responded.

"That's why the castle only appears on the mountain when the rightful king appears. It doesn't show up for just anyone!" enthused Matthew.

Mother and son got out of the car and walked up the gravel path toward the large steakhouse, holding hands as they made their way through the verdant pastures. At this point, with her belly the size it was, Maggie felt that it was her son helping her walk rather than the other way around.

Once seated, Maggie sighed. She was relieved to be off her feet. Both of them perused the menu, even though neither of them would ever consider deviating from their usual order: nachos to start and a Hawaiian steak for both.

"Can I go play outside?" Matthew requested.

"Do you know what you're going to order?"

Matthew responded with a cheeky smile.

"Same as always, huh? Ok, but don't go far, and don't take too long," admonished Maggie.

Matthew's mother hadn't even finished her sentence before he slipped away from the red leather booth and dodged a couple of waiters dressed in black and white as he bolted out the door toward the nearby green hills.

Matthew always came back exhausted after running circles around the restaurant, which is what she was hoping would happen this time too. She enjoyed hearing his fantastical stories, but they often went over her head and she became frustrated at herself for not knowing how to respond.

The large platter of nachos arrived, and Matthew was still not back. He was too young to have a phone, but he never spent longer than 10 or 15 minutes running around the pastures outside the restaurant. Luckily, Maggie's pregnancy meant she was always hungry enough to polish off whatever was in front of her.

More than 30 minutes had passed since Matthew left, which began to worry Maggie. Matthew had a proclivity to imagine impossible yet imaginative scenarios, while Maggie tended to envision the worst-case scenario for each situation.

Is he lost? Is he hurt? she wondered.

As her imagination began to get the better of her, she almost involuntarily and rather awkwardly slid out of the booth and crossed the gleaming hardwood floors as she headed out of the restaurant.

Once outside, she could not see Matthew anywhere. She called his name but heard no response.

Suddenly, her mind recalled all the articles she'd read about child abductions.

Maggie called out for her son furiously as she struggled to walk over to the nearby hills, where she hoped she would finally find him.

Although the hills were not too steep, her pregnant belly made her move slowly and awkwardly, and she had no one to hold her hand as she climbed. Maggie tried to control her thoughts, but she couldn't help herself from beginning to plan what she'd do in case she couldn't find Matthew or, worse, if she found him unconscious or injured.

Her fear spurred her to try to move faster until she finally reached the top.

Matthew was sitting at the summit of the hill, resting his back against a tall elm tree under the shade the branches provided.

"Matthew!" Maggie yelled, "do you have any idea how worried I was?!"

Before Maggie could elaborate, she noticed Matthew look up with tears in his eyes.

"The castle didn't show up for me. I'm not fit to be a king…" he sobbed.

It took a lot for Matthew to cry, so she knew he was genuinely upset. As angry and tired as she was, she couldn't bring herself to scold him further.

Maggie took a couple of deep breaths and walked over to her son.

"I was worried about you…" she began.

"I knew the castle wouldn't show up for me. I found the mountain, but not the castle…" cried Matthew.

Maggie held onto the thick branches of the tree and lowered herself to sit by her son. She struggled to find the right words to say. She could not fault him for the emotions caused by his imagination; after all, in a way, she had fallen victim to the same thing when catastrophizing possible reasons for her son's absence.

Maggie smiled as she realized that her imagination was not that far off from her son's, and they were both upset over things that were not real.

"Do you know why the castle didn't reveal itself to you?" she inquired gently.

"Why?" Matthew asked as he wiped his tears on his muddy, grass-stained jeans.

"Because you have an even bigger responsibility than being a king waiting for you," explained Maggie.

"What responsibility?"

"Being a big brother. Your little brother will need you to teach him to be brave and fight against dragons. The castle knows your brother would be lost without you; that is why it is letting you stay with us," elaborated Maggie.

Matthew smiled at his mother and then looked at her pregnant belly.

"Don't worry, little brother, I will keep you safe," Matthew declared as he wrapped his arms around his mother's belly. "I'll be your protector."

THE VISIT

Dan paced his small bedroom frantically until he realized he needed more space to pace. He walked over to the living room, which was not significantly larger but had fewer clothes on the floor. His girlfriend was away, so the apartment was messier than usual.

Great, now I'm going to have to clean up the apartment as well, Dan lamented.

His father, Sebastian Hawkes, an erudite and very financially successful businessman, was visiting him for his birthday. Initially, Dan was excited about seeing his dad after such a long time, but he was also nervous about what Sebastian would say about his lifestyle.

Sebastian was an old-fashioned man who had become very powerful through hard work and perseverance. He also believed his son could do great things if he just put his mind to it, which is exactly what Dan was trying to do.

Dan had been trying to turn his life around for the past few years. After years of frivolous living as a carefree teenager and happy-go-lucky young adult, Dan had found the love of his life and was dedicated to working as hard as possible to one day becoming as successful as his father, or at least getting close to being that successful.

***

Dan had taken the day off work from his job as a finance executive to be with his dad. During the sporadic calls he got from his father, he would inform him of how happy he was at work and how much responsibility he had. However, this wasn't strictly true. Dan was not enjoying the work as much as he thought he would and was looking for a change, but he was not ready to divulge this to his judgmental father.

During their breakfast at the coffee shop down the street, Dan's father kept questioning him about work, regardless of how hard Dan tried to change the conversation and talk about anything else.

"It's great; I'm thrilled," Dan declared as he fiddled with the paper coffee sleeve in his hands and tried to relax, readjusting his position on the green polyester sofa.

Sebastian was in his usual business attire, even though he had retired from working years ago. He loved blue, which was made apparent by his blue tie and dress shirt. He glanced around the coffee place Dan frequented with his girlfriend on the weekends, and Dan began to worry that he disapproved of the setting.

"Do you like this place?" Sebastian asked.

"I do, very much," replied Dan.

"What do you like about it?"

Dan successfully stifled a sigh of frustration.

***

The night was dark, but the city was brightly lit by the streetlights and the glowing windows of the tall buildings. There were no stars in the sky. The bustle of Friday night traffic provided the backdrop to Dan's stroll through the city with his father.

Dan zipped up his brown coat while his dad continued to walk in just a blazer, seemingly unaffected by the cold.

"What is special about your job? Why do you like working there?" Sebastian asked again.

Dan shook his head in disbelief that his father would be so brazen in his questioning; it was as if no matter what Dan did in life, his father would never approve.

"I work with people who don't judge me," Dan responded rather harshly.

"But do these people drive you to become a better version of yourself?" pestered his father.

"That's it!" Dan snapped as he turned around to face his father just before they approached the pedestrian crosswalk in front of them.

Sebastian looked at his son, bewildered. Dan could feel the anger rising in his throat.

For a brief moment, both father and son stood in silence, just looking at each other, as people loudly came in and out of the burger joint only a few feet from where they were awkwardly standing.

Dan put his hands in his pocket and looked around, unsure of what to say next.

"What's the matter?" Sebastian asked his visibly flustered son.

"Why are you so critical? You kept looking around at the coffee place I took you to this morning, and now you keep asking me why I'm happy at my job. All I ever do is try to make you proud of me, but I never will!" shouted Dan.

The light turned green, and Dan stormed across the crosswalk. When he got to the other side, he noticed his father hadn't moved from where they had previously been standing.

He knew his father would be surprised to see him react this way, but he didn't expect his face to express such bewilderment.

The light remained green and people continued to cross, oblivious to the emotional staredown happening between father and son on opposite sides of the street.

After a few more seconds of inaction, both men hastily started to cross the street at the same time until they met in the center of the crossing.

"I'm sorry," Sebastian apologized after almost bumping into his son, "I had no idea it was affecting you this way."

"I just want you to be proud of me," mumbled Dan.

"I am. I am very proud of you. That's why I've been asking you all these questions," explained Sebastian.

"What do you mean?" Dan replied incredulously.

Sebastian ushered his son back to the other side of the street to continue the conversation.

"I am finally setting up my café. It's been a dream of mine for years, and I've been putting everything in place to start getting it up and running next year."

"That's why you were so interested in the café this morning…" murmured Dan to himself.

"Yes. I want you to run the business…" Sebastian said tentatively.

"What?" Dan gasped.

"That's why I've been asking you about work. I don't want to take you away from a job that makes you happy. As much as I would like you to run this business, I only want what's best for you," his father offered.

Everything about the day with his father was now making perfect sense; however, Dan had never expected this kind of revelation.

"I've never run a business before…" muttered Dan.

"I trust you," Sebastian replied wholeheartedly.

Dan looked at his father, then at the busy street, and smiled. Regardless of his decision, his father's approval was the most important revelation of the day.

"Thank you," Dan said fervently.

In reply, Sebastian pulled his son into a heartfelt hug.

Chapter 2

Five Stories About Friendship

The Decision

Natalie had been John's friend for many years. They were inseparable, like brother and sister— only without the fighting. Natalie was a few years younger than John, but it was clear to all their mutual friends and anybody else who knew them that she was the more mature one of the two.

As close as they were, John hadn't actually seen Natalie in years. The last time he'd seen her was at the airport when he left their hometown to pursue a postgraduate degree in Spain and stayed after being offered a job there.

John was happy in Spain, but had yet to find a friend like Natalie. What he had found, however, was Laura, a girl he loved very much: so much so that he was planning to marry her one day in the not-so-distant future.

Laura was everything he dreamed of in a woman, and he would constantly talk about her to Natalie during their weekly phone calls.

However, as time passed and their relationship developed, John began noticing strange behaviors in Laura that bothered him. Laura would constantly ask John where he was, even though it was obvious he was at work. She would also get suspicious whenever he chatted with anyone on his phone.

When Natalie asked how things were going, John still very much professed his love, but found it hard to focus on anything other than Laura's blinding good looks.

"But how is the relationship going?" Natalie would insist.

"It's strange. I feel like she doesn't trust me. I am 100% faithful to her, and I don't understand why she doesn't see it," lamented John.

It was true that John was faithful, and he spent most of his days confused over the lack of trust between him and the most beautiful girl he had ever been with.

One afternoon, after John arrived home from work and was having dinner with Laura at the round wooden table in their cramped studio apartment, he got a text message from Natalie.

Much to Laura's chagrin, John opened the text and read it.

"WHAAAT?!" John exclaimed as he shot up from his seat in disbelief, almost knocking over the steak and potatoes he'd cooked for himself and Laura.

Laura's beautiful brown eyes beamed at John, unsure how to react to his unexplainable outburst.

"Natalie is coming to live here! She's also going to do a postgraduate like me!" celebrated John.

Laura's reaction was not the one John had been hoping for. In fact, it seemed like she refused to react at all.

"Why?" she asked, looking down at her food as if she had found a hair in it.

**

As trepidated as John was over Laura's jealous behavior, he never would have expected her to have such a big problem with Natalie's arrival in Spain.

As the day John was due to pick up Natalie from the airport drew nearer, the tension between

John and Laura reached its boiling point. They were fighting so much that Laura decided to go on a yoga trip with her ex-boyfriend.

"So, I can't hang out with my best friend, but you can go on a yoga retreat with your ex-boyfriend?" steamed John.

"He's the instructor!" Laura would yell. The same fight happened repeatedly until Laura eventually left for her yoga retreat the night before Natalie was due to arrive, leaving John alone in the apartment.

When morning came, John got up and excitedly raced to the airport. As happy as he felt, he was also saddened by the tension in his relationship with Laura.

The reunion between John and Natalie turned heads at the airport, making many people believe that the grinning girl John was embracing was his girlfriend.

After the airport, John took Natalie to the café where he and Laura often went on Sundays.

"So, how are things going?" Natalie asked.

John explained everything to his best friend, who was immediately concerned by how clear it was that Laura and John's relationship was causing John a lot of sadness and worry.

They talked for almost two hours before Natalie invited John to stay over at the small apartment she was renting so that he wouldn't have to be alone.

John agreed to stay with Natalie, although he had no idea how he would break the news to Laura.

***

On the last day that John was staying with Natalie, a couple of days before Laura arrived back from her yoga trip, John got a call from his mother. They spoke about many things, and John told her that he was staying with Natalie at her apartment.

"But she was supposed to be on an induction trip with her future classmates this weekend. She was so excited about going!" John's mother said.

"She was?" John asked, dumbfounded.

Once the conversation ended, John confronted Natalie about the trip.

"Is it true?" he asked.

Natalie nodded.

"You missed out on that for me? And you weren't going to tell me about it?"

Natalie nodded again.

"I knew you were in pain, so I wanted to be there for you," she said simply.

John didn't know what to say. He contemplated the difference between Natalie's decision to stay home to help him feel better and

Laura's decision to leave on a yoga trip with her ex-boyfriend.

It didn't take long before things became very clear to John, which made him smile.

"Can I stay here a little longer?" he asked softly.

"Of course! How much longer?" Natalie said, grinning.

"A couple of weeks. Depends on how long it takes for either Laura or I to move out."

"Move out?" Natalie asked in astonishment, putting down her white coffee mug a little too hard and sloshing coffee onto the table.

"If I look at the difference between what you chose to do for me this week and what Laura did by leaving me to go on a yoga retreat with her ex-boyfriend, regardless of if he is the instructor or not, the distinction is clear. I should be with someone who's there for me and doesn't abandon me out of jealousy," John explained.

Natalie smiled. Her green eyes contentedly rested on John's determined smile.

John ended up staying much longer than a couple of weeks. He finally moved out a year later—but with Natalie, as they found another apartment together and began to build the life that they continue to share to this day.

THE REUNION

Diego hated the idea of going to his high school reunion.

"It's going to be fine!" his fiancée Deborah insisted from their en suite bathroom as she did her hair in front of the oval-shaped mirror.

"It's not going to be fine. I don't know why I let you convince me to do these things!" Diego protested as he sat on the double bed and tied the shoelaces of his favorite brown leather shoes, which he only wore on special occasions.

"Because deep down, you know that you'll regret not going. It's been ten years; surely it will be nice to see your friends again!" countered Deborah.

"I was only there for two years. I hardly even remember anyone!" insisted Diego.

That statement wasn't strictly true.

One of the main reasons Diego felt flustered about attending his high school reunion was that he had been bullied for those final two years of school.

As a high schooler, Diego was a hypersensitive and introverted kid who found it very hard to relate to others. People sometimes wondered if perhaps he was autistic, but it was just a case of Diego constantly moving to different countries due to his father's job. He'd never been able to develop any close friendships, and therefore had missed the necessary social skills to survive high school.

Diego turned around to look at his fiancée as she got ready. Diego and Deborah had been engaged for a year and a half, and all his thoughts of starting to plan their wedding were put on hold over the anxiety he was feeling about the reunion.

"I don't know if I should go. Maybe you go without me, honey…" Diego suggested.

"It's YOUR high school reunion!" Deborah retorted as she exited the bathroom and switched off the lights. She sat next to her fiancé and held his hand. She was wearing the gold and silver watch he'd gotten her for her last birthday, which she only wore on special occasions.

Deborah put her arm around her fiancé and lowered her head to meet his worried expression.

"It's going to be ok. Let yourself be surprised," she said softly.

***

The first person Diego noticed at the reunion was his old acquaintance Greg. Greg had always been popular. He was tall, good-looking, and girls had always been interested in him back in high school.

With Diego's recent promotion and engagement to Deborah, he felt he had a lot to be proud of, but he was worried his achievements would be undermined by Greg—just like everyone had undermined Diego's accomplishments back in school.

Greg noticed Diego and immediately honed in on him like a missile.

"It's so good to see you, D!" Greg exclaimed as he surveyed Diego quickly. "You look great!"

Diego and Greg continued to make small talk until Diego decided to get another drink.

***

After a couple hours, Diego had had a little too much to drink and was finally starting to feel comfortable talking to classmates he'd known back in the day.

From the corner of his eye, he saw Greg signaling Deborah to come speak to him, which seemed very odd.

Diego watched his fiancée walk over to Greg as he began to whisper things in her ear.

"What's going on there?" Diego asked as he looked at his fiancée speaking to Greg in such close proximity.

"Maybe Greg is up to his old ways with that absolute beauty…" one of Diego's classmates asserted as he took a sip of his champagne, unaware that the "absolute beauty" he was referring to was Diego's fiancée.

Rather than inform his old classmate that he was speaking about Diego's fiancée, Diego continued to assess the situation.

After a couple minutes, Diego turned to check on Deborah and Greg once more, but he could not find either his fiancée or Greg, which prompted him to go looking for them.

He found Greg and Deborah talking, their heads very close together, behind one of the room's large columns.

"What's going on here?!" Diego demanded as he pushed his way between them. "Are you chatting up my fiancée?"

Diego got really close to Greg's face (or chin, rather).

"Honey!" Deborah called out.

"Why are you hiding from me and talking to this guy?!" challenged Diego.

"D, calm down…." Greg began.

"No! You stole all my girlfriends in school and I won't let you do it again!" growled Diego.

"Diego, he was asking me how to approach you about asking for business advice and if you could help him professionally!" Deborah explained, looking frustrated and slightly embarrassed.

"What?" Diego inquired, dumbfounded.

"I'm so sorry, D. I just heard how successful you were these days, and I was wondering if there was a chance you could help me. I haven't been doing so good lately ever since I was fired from the garage…" mumbled Greg.

Diego took a couple deep breaths and looked at his fiancée before backing away from Greg in shame.

"I'm really sorry, Greg. I had no idea…" he started.

"It's ok. I'm sorry for being an idiot back in the day. You have every right to be mad," Greg admitted.

Diego looked up at Greg and felt a wave of sympathy flow through him. Luckily, not too many people noticed the altercation.

"You wanna go have a drink and talk business?" Diego asked.

Greg's face lit up immediately, and the two men headed off to refresh their drinks.

BUCKLEY AND BAILEY

Buckley was the second dog I'd ever had. The first had been a golden retriever when I was very young, too young to feel any ownership over a dog that belonged to the entire family more than it did to me. It had been my older brother who had petitioned to get a dog back then. But this time I was living alone, and I could say without a shadow of a doubt that Buckley was my dog.

It took almost half a year to find the right dog for me. I found the breed I liked fairly quickly, but finding a Stabyhoun breeder near me was a challenge. I was living in Europe at the time, and Stabyhouns are a Dutch breed, but I was living in Spain and the only way to get a Stabyhoun was to live either in the Netherlands or England.

However, after about a month spent trying to find a way to get one of these beautiful dogs, I spoke to my brother, who lived in Germany and said there was a Stabyhoun breeder near him.

I hadn't spoken to my brother in many years due to a falling-out, which upset my parents, but I knew that if I tried to force the relationship we would only be making matters worse. The only reason we spoke this time was that my parents had informed him of what I was searching for, and—after what I imagined took a lot of coercion and convincing from my parents—he reached out to me and told me about the breeder.

Long story short, I took my remote job abroad to Germany for a while to get Buckley.

I spoke no German and had visited the country a couple of times as a child, but never stayed longer than a week. In fact, I once visited

Germany with my parents and the golden retriever we had back then.

I moved about an hour away from my brother, and although I told my parents that I would gladly visit him or that I would be happy to have him stay with me for a while, I was correct in assuming that that would not happen.

The connection between Buckley and me was not instant. However, once I spent enough time with him, I found myself missing—and often needing—his presence. It became clear that I was genuinely falling in love with the little guy.

I was due to stay in Germany for six months before returning to Spain with Buckley. I enrolled myself in an immersive German-language course, and during those classes, I met a girl named Anne. Anne was American and had a dog, a three-year-old German Shepherd named Bailey, who was almost bigger than she was.

We took our dogs on our first date. They were particularly tired that day and did not interact with each other very much. We continued to see each other almost every day, and eventually, I moved into Anne's apartment, which was bigger and better located than mine.

I did not know what my plans were now that Anne was in my life, but that was something I would contemplate during the months I had left in Germany. However, a couple of weeks after moving in with Anne, I began to feel highly frustrated with how Bailey would behave around Buckley.

I was unsure if something had changed, or if I had just previously been unaware of this behavior between the two dogs. Still, Bailey was much more territorial and temperamental than Buckley.

My blood would boil whenever Bailey barked at Buckley for taking his toy or going outside to the terrace where Bailey was sunbathing. Things never got past the point of barking. Still, the issue was that Buckley didn't bark at any other dogs, so I was afraid Bailey's aggressive behavior would negatively affect Buckley's serene and passive nature or that, eventually, the situation would escalate.

The dogs' interaction quickly became a point of contention between Anne and I. Anne proclaimed that this was normal behavior and the two dogs loved each other. Still, my overprotective nature made it difficult for me to accept that.

My parents kept trying to persuade me to reach out to my older brother for advice since, for the past seven years, he'd had two dogs and was more knowledgeable on these matters than I was, but I was still reluctant to speak to him.

One day, Anne and I took the dogs to the park for some exercise. Anne and I were sitting on a bench arguing yet again about me thinking that Bailey needed an attitude adjustment while she maintained that the problem only existed in my mind.

At one point, a huge dog—even bigger than Bailey—began chasing Buckley around the park. Suddenly, I saw Buckley stop running and recoil in fear as the large dog continued to bark and snap at him.

Before I could react, Bailey ran to Buckley's defense and began barking at the larger dog. The two got so loud and close to each other that everyone noticed and a commotion erupted. Luckily, the owner of the larger dog arrived in time and pulled his dog away from the scene.

When Anne and I got home, we found a little blood coming out of Buckley's thigh, which must have been from the incident at the dog park. Thankfully, the cut was not deep, and we knew it would heal without a trip to the vet.

I spent the rest of the afternoon sitting alone in the kitchen, pondering my worries about

Buckley and Bailey. Suddenly, I received a text message from Anne asking me to come to the living room, which I did. Once I got there, Anne had her index finger pressed against her lips. She signaled me to be quiet and to follow her.

Anne led me to the bedroom where Bailey's large bed was located. On the bed was Buckley, taking up about 10% of the bed, with Bailey lying just off the bed next to Buckley's head. Bailey had wedged himself in the little space in the corner of the room and was licking Buckley's head; Buckley was either fast asleep, or about to be.

I watched the two of them and immediately knew that Bailey was comforting his brother and that it was working. I also appreciated how Bailey had stood up for Buckley at the dog park against the aggressive dog.

As Anne and I stood together, we witnessed Buckley waking up and putting his head on top of Bailey's, which was both funny and endearing.

The next day I apologized to Anne and explained to her that I had been wrong to doubt the loyalty and love between the two dogs. Anne smiled.

"I think there's one more person you need to consider in this realization of yours…" she said.

About an hour later, I called my brother to ask about visiting him. He insisted I bring Anne and the dogs. I smiled, filled with joy at the thought.

THE TREE

Fabienne and Anna were best friends and completely inseparable. They had been in the same class for the past four years of elementary school and were excited about spending the summer vacation together.

Every summer, they would venture into the woods and climb their favorite oak tree, which technically was in a backyard belonging to an older lady who never left her house and never bothered anyone.

Last summer, they'd built a swing around one of the branches and carved their initials into the bark. This year, they were determined to build a tree house, something they'd been dreaming of doing for a long time, but they were advised against it since the tree was the older lady's property, after all.

"But no one even knows her name!" Anna protested to her mother.

"Her name is Tamara, and she is a very kind woman," replied her mother.

"I've heard she's an evil witch. Witches should not be allowed to have nice trees!" Fabienne joined in.

Anna's mother shook her head in disapproval and sent them on their way to the forest; she knew once they joined forces, there was no stopping them.

Once they arrived at the tree, they began circling it to imagine how they wanted the tree house to look.

"I think it should be pink, and boys shouldn't ever be allowed!" Anna declared as she looked up at the prodigious branches.

Fabienne tore her gaze away from the tree and shot a look of disapproval toward her best friend.

"No boys?" she asked skeptically.

"Yeah, only girls…" insisted Anna.

"What about the boys we like?" countered Fabienne.

"Not even them!"

Fabienne was visibly displeased by this suggestion.

"What if I want to bring my little brother?" she asked.

"Not even him," Anna retorted.

"What if I want the treehouse to be blue?" contended Fabienne.

The discussion ensued to the point where both girls became frustrated with each other and began fighting for the first time since they'd known each other.

The fighting got so loud that it even attracted the attention of the mysterious old lady who lived in the decrepit house nearby.

Her appearance shocked Fabienne and Anna into silence.

"What are your names, young ladies?" Tamara asked as she beckoned them over.

"I'm Fabienne, and she is Anna..." supplied Fabienne hesitantly.

"Then you are the two girls who have been damaging my tree with your carvings. That tree is beautiful and should be preserved and treated respectfully," commented Tamara.

The two girls apologized.

"You're going to have to make it up to me. I want you to rake the leaves off my front yard and weed my garden beds every morning for ten days. If you do that, I won't tell your parents about what you've done," said Tamara.

***

To both Fabienne's and Anna's surprise, Anna's mother ultimately agreed with Tamara.

"I warned you, girls. Now you have to face the consequences!" she admonished.

As the days passed, Anna and Fabienne silently raked the leaves and worked in Tamara's garden. They refused to speak to each other the entire time they were there, which was about an hour each day.

This uncomfortable situation continued for most of the time they were forced to clean up Tamara's yard and garden.

Finally, on the last day, Anna broke the uncomfortable silence they were getting so accustomed to.

"You can bring your brother to the tree house if you want. And we can paint it blue if you want," she offered shyly.

Fabienne looked surprised but felt compelled to reply.

"Thank you. I think pink would be a nice color for the treehouse…" she said hesitantly.

"Maybe we can find a color we both like… what do you think about yellow?" asked Anna.

"I would LOVE yellow!" Fabienne exclaimed.

'We're going to have to find another tree to build it in, though…" mused Anna.

After a couple of minutes, the girls continued to talk like nothing had happened. They were right back to where they had left off before the argument. They began enjoying each others' company so much again that they were disheartened when the chores ended and they could no longer clean Tamara's garden.

As they finished up, Tamara came outside and announced, "You did well. I am very proud of you girls."

"We're sorry for damaging your tree; we won't do it again," chorused the girls.

"What do you mean? I thought you were going to build a treehouse," said Tamara.

Fabienne and Anna looked at each other, befuddled.

"I thought you didn't want us near the tree anymore…" Anna inquired.

"All I wanted was for you two to stop fighting and remember how much you love being friends.

And look, my plan worked. You have my blessing to build a treehouse," declared Tamara.

Anna and Fabienne ran up to Tamara and hugged her simultaneously.

Later, they ran home, excited to tell Anna's mother what had just happened. Once they did, Anna's mother laughed and confessed that she knew about the plan all along because Tamara had called her and explained everything.

"Just never forget what you mean to each other. It's one thing to carve it on a tree; it's another to work at the friendship every day, even when times are tough," Anna's mother reminded both girls before walking back to the kitchen to get them some well-deserved snacks.

SHOW-AND-TELL

It was show-and-tell day at school, and Zachary was excited about showing his dinosaur toy his father had gotten him during one of his business trips.

However, Zachary was not excited about having to escort the new kid, Tony, through the school campus yet again. Tony had just been enrolled a couple of days ago, and Zachary had been assigned to be his chaperone for the week.

The problem wasn't so much the chaperoning, but the fact that Tony seemed to be a very strange boy who didn't like to talk or interact with others.

Zachary was the complete opposite. Zachary had always been the loudest, most extroverted boy in class—the one everybody wanted to play with, which might have been the reason why they thought he would be the best choice to guide the new boy around the school.

The problem was that for the last couple of days, ever since Zachary had been spending time with Tony like he'd been instructed to do, the other kids who usually loved playing with Zachary had been keeping their distance. In Zachary's mind, the problem was obviously Tony.

"I brought a drawing I did for show-and-tell," Tony declared worriedly as he walked through the halls alongside Zachary, "but I don't know if the other kids will like it."

"You'll be ok, so don't worry about it. Everyone is going to be paying attention to my toy anyway…" boasted Zachary.

"What did you bring?" asked Tony.

"I brought a T-Rex; my father got it for me, and it's red!" bragged Zachary.

"Can I see it?" Tony said.

"You'll see it in class when I show it. Everyone is going to love it," Zachary declared.

Zachary walked down the halls with his chest held high, but he was still worried that Tony being next to him was keeping everyone else away from him.

"Are you sure people are going to like my drawing?" Tony asked.

"They're going to love it. Don't worry about it," answered Zachary.

"Thank you," said Tony.

The time finally came for show-and-tell, and all the kids sat on the multicolored carpet excitedly as they anxiously waited for show-and-tell to begin.

Because of Tony's last name, he was due to be one of the first ones presenting, but he declared that he wanted to go after Zachary. That made Zachary cringe with embarrassment.

As the children took their turns for show-and-tell, they enthusiastically presented their various objects and artifacts in great detail. One child had even brought a live tarantula, which he kept as a pet at home.

"My dinosaur is way cooler than that spider!" whispered Zachary.

"I'm sure it is!" Tony responded.

"Are you sure you want to go after me? Maybe going a few before me would be better…" suggested Zachary.

"I'm scared. I'd rather go after you if that's ok," said Tony.

"That's fine," Zachary reluctantly accepted.

It was finally Zachary's turn to present. He noticed several children around him begin whispering and smiling as he got up and walked over to his backpack to retrieve the dinosaur. Once the sizable red T-rex was in his hands, he ran over to stand next to the teacher on her wooden stool in front of the semicircle of children.

Children were already smiling and giggling among each other, which Zachary took as a good sign at first. At this point, he was glad to finally be separated from Tony.

"This is Rexy," Zachary began, "I've had him for about a year now, and he is my favorite dinosaur. They did not have a lot of red dinosaurs in the store where my father was, so he got this one because he knew it was special."

As Zachary continued talking, the murmurs and the giggles got louder, so much so that the teacher had to tell everyone to quiet down. Tony was the only person paying attention to Zachary instead of laughing.

The commotion continued despite the teacher's protestations, which made Zachary feel progressively more uncomfortable. The only thing that calmed his nerves was looking at how attentive Tony was throughout his show-and-tell.

"Can we call you dinosaur boy?" a boy cried out, which gave way to rapturous laughter from the other children.

Zachary became overwhelmed with shame and humiliation as the teacher tried to calm the children. Zachary promptly finished his show-and-tell and sat beside Tony, feeling deflated and defeated.

"Tony, you're next," the teacher called out.

Zachary was too busy looking down at the ground to notice Tony take his dinosaur from him and take it with him as he took his place in front of the classroom.

"Today, I want to talk about my friend Zachary," Tony declared, which caught Zachary's attention and prompted him to finally look up.

"When I first arrived here, I was very nervous. Zachary was with me the entire time, and he answered all my questions and helped me feel better. I think he is a great friend, and I'm very happy he has helped me feel better," explained Tony.

Tony continued to describe how thankful he was to Zachary as he held the dinosaur in his hand. This time, nobody laughed or even made any sound; it was clear that Tony was speaking from the heart. His words were especially poignant considering this was the first time anyone other than Zachary had heard him speak.

Once the presentation finished, the students clapped as Tony sat beside his friend.

Zachary smiled and no longer felt ashamed to be sitting next to Tony; in fact, he felt quite the opposite.

Once class finished, Zachary and Tony walked to recess together and have been doing so as best friends ever since.

Chapter 3

Five Stories About Love

Balto

Joey knew that Flo loved dogs. The truth is, Joey loved dogs too, but he had never considered getting one himself. Sure, whenever there was a dog around—either at a friend's house or perhaps in a restaurant near his table—he loved being around the dog and playing with it, but the thought of getting a dog of his own had never crossed his mind until about a month ago, when he was talking to his ex-girlfriend Flo.

Joey and Flo had broken up a couple of months ago due to all the fighting they'd been doing, but after about a week of silence, they decided to talk again and see if they could work things out.

It had been Flo who had suggested taking things slowly instead of getting back together right away. She thought they should see if it was a good idea to reunite without any idea of how to avoid continuing to fight in such an impassioned way.

While Joey could see she was right, he felt miserable without her. Every day that passed made him feel more certain that breaking up was a mistake.

After some time deliberating what would be the best way to get Flo back, Joey came up with the notion of getting a dog. Flo had always wanted a dog, and he had never seen her get more excited than when a dog was in her general vicinity.

The original plan was to surprise Flo with a puppy that would initially live with Joey but could also spend time at Flo's place, since they lived so close to each other. Joey even contemplated insisting that the dog live with him the whole time, thinking that might be an effective way of getting Flo to move in with him—which he'd wanted her to do for some time.

As it turned out, getting a puppy was nowhere near as easy as Joey thought it would be. Joey tried many different kennels, but they always seemed to have an endless waiting list. Finally, he found one with a newborn chocolate labrador puppy.

Joey went to see the puppy and knew that Flo would love it.

"He's a little meatball!" Joey exclaimed to the woman as she handed him a chubby and excitable three-month-old puppy. His eyes were yellow and full of character. Although he was very young, he was heavier than Joey had expected.

"You are a chubby little guy, aren't you?" Joey asked what could potentially be his new dog.

The puppy wagged his tail enthusiastically, and as he did, Joey decided that this was the one.

"I'm gonna call you Balto," he informed the puppy in his hands, smiling broadly.

When he got home, he could not contain his excitement. He immediately told Flo all about the puppy, and she reacted just as joyfully as he'd hoped.

***

A couple of days before Joey was due to pick up Balto from the kennel, he and Flo had yet another fight. This one was more heated than any fight they'd ever had before, leading Flo to declare that there was no way they could get back together.

Joey did not get much sleep after that incident, so he showed up to pick up Balto with bags under his eyes and dragging his limbs a bit. However, once he was handed Balto, he quickly realized he needed to wake up, as the newborn pup behaved as if he had had all the sleep in the world and was ready to take on the world.

Joey struggled to keep the brown puppy in his arms as he headed to the car and drove home.

To make matters worse, raising Balto did not allow Joey to catch up on any of the sleep he'd missed worrying about what had happened with Flo. He hadn't even managed to tell her about Balto. However, as the days passed, Joey found it impossible to think about anything other than Balto.

Joey was waking up every three hours to let him out and spent the rest of his time running around cleaning up whatever mess Balto had made in the two minutes Joey went to the bathroom.

The first week was very taxing for Joey. One day, after Joey had been standing outside in the pouring rain for 20 minutes with Balto so that he could go to the bathroom on the grass, Joey gave up and headed back inside. Almost immediately, Balto squatted on the welcome mat by the front door and went to the bathroom in the house.

Joey screamed as loud as he could, which made Balto squeal in fear and run away from him.

Once he collected himself, Joey searched for Balto for a long time before he finally found him hiding under the dining table.

"I'm so sorry, Balto. I will never scream at you that way again," Joey promised.

After that incident, Joey went for a walk through the woods with Balto and realized that in the entire time that Balto had been at the house, he had never once thought about Flo. As sleep-deprived and frustrated as he was, at least he was no longer obsessing over Flo the way he thought he would be; his mind was too focused on Balto.

Almost a year later, Flo reached out to Joey. He got her call when he was at the dog beach with Balto. Flo asked Joey if they could talk about maybe getting back together after all.

Joey couldn't believe it. He had dreamed about getting this call from Flo one day, but for some reason, he did not feel as euphoric or excited as he had imagined he would.

Balto was chasing his canine friends all around the beach. Joey had kept his promise to Balto and never screamed at him again; in fact, he had never felt the same need to scream ever since that promise was made.

"I'm sorry, Flo, but I don't know if we will be able to stop being so aggressive to each other, and I promised Balto that I would never let him see me scream ever again," he finally said.

This response shocked Flo. She insisted that Joey reconsider his decision, but he couldn't.

Once the phone call ended, Joey opened his arms and contracted his core to prepare for Balto as the dog ran toward him as fast as he could and leaped into his arms. Joey hugged Balto and kissed the top of his head.

"It's you and I forever, buddy," Joey said as he looked into Balto's yellow eyes. "Thank you for everything."

MARIE

It had been a couple of weeks since Joey had rejected Flo's petition to get back together. Although he was initially confident that he had made the right choice, he eventually began to doubt whether he had inadvertently made a mistake and might have lost his chance to be with the woman he was truly supposed to be with.

The more people Joey spoke to about the uncertainty he felt, the more he heard about how it was normal to feel doubt. Although Joey believed those voices to be right in their assessment of the situation, he was still riddled with doubt.

One particularly dark and gloomy day, which fitted Joey's tormented state of mind, he headed to the dog beach with Balto to think about his situation.

Once there, he spotted a red-haired girl with a cocker spaniel who refused to get into the water no matter how hard she tried to get him to join her for a swim.

It didn't take long for Joey to approach her and start giving her advice on how to get her dog to stop being scared of the water.

"I'm a dog trainer," she informed Joey as she tried her best not to giggle.

After a couple of minutes of playful banter, the two exchanged numbers and arranged to meet the following day for lunch. The girl's name was Marie.

Both Joey and Marie brought their dogs to lunch, and to Joey's exultation, the dogs became immediate friends.

The date went very well, except for an unfortunate incident involving Joey spilling water on his white shirt, but he played it off as a joke and made Marie laugh in a way that he appreciated.

After the date, Joey dropped Marie off at her apartment and kissed her on the cheek before she stepped out of the car and grabbed her dog from the back seat.

Joey went to bed that night happy, replaying the date in his head over and over until he fell asleep thinking about it.

The following day, Joey woke up late, but he saw he had a disturbingly lengthy message from Marie on his phone. Still in bed and only half awake, he read Marie's confession that she was due to leave the country in 24 hours to return to Germany, where she was from, and that she hadn't mentioned it before because she was having such a lovely date.

Joey called Marie immediately and arranged to meet her for coffee that afternoon.

During their second encounter, Marie apologized profusely and explained why she was too scared to tell Joey the truth.

"Is there any way that you could stay a little longer?" Joey asked.

"I would need a place to stay, and I would need to tell my parents. They would have so many questions," she said hesitantly.

Joey and Marie continued to discuss the matter until Joey realized what he had to do.

"I won't let you go. If you want, you can stay with Balto and me, but I can't let you go like this," he declared.

Marie smiled at Joey as if that was exactly what she had wanted to hear all along.

"Ok. I will stay," she agreed.

Marie and her small dog stayed an extra week. She temporarily moved in with Joey and Balto, and the four of them went sightseeing and on long walks almost every day.

When it came time for Marie to return home, she hugged and kissed Joey as if it was the last time she would see him.

"Call me when you land," Joey told Marie.

Once Marie landed safely and was back at home with her parents, she called Joey, and they spoke all day on the phone. They continued to speak virtually every day that week until Joey built up the courage to ask Marie to be his girlfriend. She accepted gleefully.

Joey ended up moving to Germany with Balto to be with Marie, and he lived there for three years until the relationship ended.

Joey moved back home with Balto after those three years but never stopped loving Marie. He still talks to her from time to time, but misses her every day.

When it has been a particularly tough day or something happens that makes him think of Marie, he calls her and reminds her what he told her that day after their first date when they discussed what she revealed to him about having to fly back to Germany.

"That day, I told you I wouldn't let you go. I want you to know that all these years later, it's still true, and my heart will never let you go," Joey told Marie, who cried and told him she felt the same.

Sometimes the most beautiful and invigorating relationships do not last forever, or at least they don't last outside of our hearts, but that does not mean that they are any less important than the ones that do.

Joey still visits the dog beach to this day, and every time he does, he thinks of Marie and no one else.

BIRTHDAY WEEK

Anne could tell that I was upset.

"What's wrong?" she asked once I hung up after talking to my parents.

Anne and I lived together in a small apartment about a four-hour drive away from my parents and most of my extended family.

"They originally said they would be here tomorrow, but now they're saying they can't make the drive until next week," I told her.

"How come?" she inquired.

"They said it's because my dad has a medical appointment they had forgotten about. I don't understand how they can do this just one day before they are due to get here," I complained.

Anne and I had spent the entire weekend buying groceries for all the meals we were planning to cook for my parents, and Anne had spent the majority of the past two days cleaning the apartment. She'd worked so hard that I was barely allowed to even get a drink of water just to preserve how immaculate she wanted to keep it.

"This is typical!" I protested as I sat at the round, wooden kitchen table, which had never gleamed the way it did then.

I somewhat aggressively slammed down my favorite white porcelain coffee mug on the table. Anne shot me a look of disapproval, which quickly communicated to me that there was something I was doing wrong. At first, I thought she disapproved of my mild outburst, but then I quickly realized the problem. I grunted and promptly grabbed a cork coaster to place under the mug so the integrity of the table she had worked so tirelessly to clean remained intact.

Anne looked content. She walked over to the table and sat next to me. She put her hand on my leg and looked at me. Her green eyes always looked their best when the sun shone upon them and highlighted the freckles surrounding them, which was the case on that particular morning.

"You have to be more patient. You know your parents love you, and that's what matters. You only know half of the story…" Anne suggested in her faint German accent, which always rose to the surface when she was speaking from the heart or she was worried about me.

"That's the problem; they didn't even want to tell me what the appointment was about or why they forgot. They just seemed so uninterested in providing context. Now we'll have to buy all these groceries and clean the apartment all over again for when they actually do come… if they ever do!" I complained.

"Well, that gives you a chance to help out with the cleaning next time," Anne proposed as she brushed her ginger hair back with a smile. I smiled, too.

For the rest of the day, my parents continued trying to get in touch with me, but I kept brushing them off, telling them I was too busy to talk. In reality, though, I was just upset that they had done exactly what I had predicted they would do: cancel at the last minute.

Finally, while I was lying on the green sofa in the living room with Anne later that day, I got a message from my parents saying that they would be there early the next morning.

"Ok, you clean the bathroom. I'll do the kitchen!" Anne exclaimed as she shot up so quickly that her blue flannel pajama pants almost fell off.

I glanced at the kitchen to my right, which was still so clean you could perform invasive surgery on the table, and chuckled. It was amazing how much importance Anne gave to ensuring a clean apartment for her in-laws and how nothing they ever did could detract from that.

***

It was the fourth day of my parents visiting Anne and me, and only two days until my actual birthday. Everything had been going well, until things blew up that evening.

While I was out running errands that evening, I got a call from my mother informing me that she had forgotten an important document back home and had to drive back with my dad.

"So you're leaving now and you won't be here for my actual birthday?" I asked.

"We will do our best!" she replied.

The conversation turned hostile, and I hung up the phone in anger. When I got home, Anne did her best to comfort me. We sat together on the sofa as she stroked my head, which normally always calmed me down but didn't work this time.

"I can't believe they are canceling yet again!" I steamed.

"They did come here, though!" Anne reminded me.

"Yes, but they aren't going to be here for my actual birthday. What frustrates me the most is that I am always right when I predict these things will happen!"

My phone continued to ring as my parents called me repeatedly, but I refused to answer.

Anna looked at me in a way that made it obvious many conflicting thoughts were running through her brain. I waited silently to see if she would share whatever was troubling her.

"There's something I'm not supposed to tell you, but I feel like I have to at this point..." she finally said.

"What is it?" I grumbled.

Anne hesitated to reveal what was on her mind, but then acquiesced to her own desire to divulge some truth I was unaware of.

"Your parents were on their way to pick up your uncles, aunts, and cousins to bring them here to surprise you..." she admitted.

"What?!" I exclaimed.

"They managed to get the confirmation from everyone right after they got to our place, and since they have the biggest car and know how to navigate city traffic the best, they'd planned on picking everyone up to drive them here," she shared.

"And now they're not coming back? Because of what I did?!"

"They are. Your parents are driving back home tonight, and tomorrow morning they will drive back here with everyone else. They wanted to surprise you," she reassured me.

I looked at Anne in disbelief. I felt like a terrible son. My immediate reaction was to call my parents and apologize for everything, but Anne stopped me.

"I have an idea," she said.

***

Anne and I quickly changed from our pajamas into regular clothes and packed our bags. We hopped in the car and headed towards the highway. I called my parents while Anne drove.

After about half an hour spent apologizing, I informed them that we were driving to their house that evening and that we would be celebrating my birthday back home.

"I'm so sorry; I didn't know the whole picture. Anne told me, but I still haven't learned to accept that she's always right," I said remorsefully.

Anne smiled.

We drove all the way to their home that night, and Anne and I slept in my childhood bedroom. The following day, Anne and I woke up to the sound of all my aunts, uncles, and cousins arguing downstairs in my parents' kitchen about what to make for breakfast.

"See where I get it from?" I jokingly asked Anne, who smiled in bed next to me.

THE PETER PAN STATUE

I was reeling from the graduation ceremony I had just left. I had finished my master's degree and was enjoying how proud my parents were of me, which did not happen as often as I would have liked.

I was also thrilled to finally be back in London. I had completed my master's almost two years ago but was only now attending my graduation ceremony. I had been away working, but I had constantly daydreamed about returning to my favorite city in the world—and now it was finally happening, and for the best reason possible.

After leaving the university my parents and I went to dinner, where they repeatedly asked me about Carole. Carole was the girlfriend I had been living with during my studies in London. Our relationship had lasted for a little under two years, and she was the person who was responsible for pushing me to complete my master's.

As much as I loved Carole when we were together, my parents might have loved her even more. Carole was a kind, intelligent, and beautiful girl who always supported me and showed me the right way to go about my problems.

Carole and I tried to make a long-distance relationship work when I left London, but it was too hard. Furthermore, when I left she could no longer afford to live in central London and she had to move back in with her parents, which always made me feel guilty for leaving.

I didn't tell my parents that when I had left London two years beforehand, Carole and I had made a deal that if we were truly meant to be, we would meet by the Peter Pan statue in Hyde Park on the seventh day of the seventh month at seven in the evening.

A couple of weeks after the ceremony, I made my way over to Hyde Park, expecting to see Carole there. I had avoided talking to her during my visit because I wanted to see if she would show up at the statue without knowing I was already in the country.

I was very excited, but equally nervous. If she showed up, it would be a very romantic story that we could tell for the rest of our lives. If she were not there, that would be very disheartening, considering that I managed to make it even though it required that I get on a plane to get there. Granted, I was already in the city for my graduation—but I like to think that even without that excuse, I would have shown up.

What was unclear was what the implications of our meeting up would be. Even if we both showed up and got back together, how would we make the relationship work when I would still eventually need to fly back to where I was living?

I also wondered if she perhaps was angry at me for leaving. Carole had a very conflicted relationship with her parents, and moving back in with them once I left was something she was unwillingly forced into due to the high cost of living in London. I worried that maybe living with her parents all this time had changed her and somehow made her less interested in seeing me or following through with romantic gestures.

As I entered Hyde Park, I looked around at all the families and friends spending time under the warm summer sun and contemplated the crazy situation I was in. I looked at my watch and noticed it was already seven, so I began walking a little faster, dodging pigeons, squirrels, and sprinting children in the process.

It did not take long for me to realize that I was wrong in thinking I'd be able to find the statue. I was already terrible at directions, and I had only visited Hyde Park once before with Carole. It was quite a voyage to get there, which meant that my foolish belief that I would be able to remember the way to where we had agreed to meet was a mistake.

I ran around the park so much that I felt I was doing more exercise than the litany of joggers out for their evening run. I stopped to get some air and to look at my watch. It was fifteen minutes past seven, and I had no idea where to find the statue.

I asked someone for directions, and they told me I wasn't even close to the statue. Once the person finally stopped explaining what paths to take and where to turn, I sprinted as fast as possible to where he indicated I had to go.

I finally arrived at the statue with sweat pouring down my face. I was half an hour late, but even more disheartening was that I could not see Carole anywhere.

I sat down on a nearby bench and waited. Perhaps she had come and gone? Had I ruined the romantic gesture?

It did not take long for me to start kicking myself in frustration.

"Excuse me?" a short, red-haired girl with glasses asked me.

"Yes?" I responded.

"Are you Joel?" she inquired.

"Yes, I am," I replied worriedly.

The girl smiled and informed me she had been sent to the statue on Carole's behalf.

"Why?" I asked.

"She was too scared about what she would feel if you didn't show up and broke her heart. And she told me to wait a long while because she knew you would get lost," the girl said.

"So she isn't here?" I asked.

"She's home, but can be here in two minutes," answered the girl.

"Two minutes?" I repeated.

"Yes. We live two minutes away. I'm her roommate," she explained.

Roommate. Upon hearing that Carole was living in central London once more and had remembered our rendezvous at the statue, I experienced a joy even greater than the one I had felt when receiving my master's diploma.

I smiled and waited as the girl excitedly informed Carole I was there. I looked up at the Peter Pan statue and felt an immense sense of gratitude that Carole still had a heart that was open enough for her to be scared of it getting hurt.

The next time I left the country was ten years later, with Carole by my side as my wife.

CAMILLA

Camilla had blonde hair and blue eyes. She was French, but spoke English with an enchanting British accent because she had studied in England for both her bachelor's and postgraduate degrees.

I couldn't remember what she had studied, but it must have been something important since right after graduation, she was employed by one of the most famous and reputable fashion houses in the world.

I, on the other hand, was still struggling to find work after graduation. I was staying at the house of a very wealthy friend who was out of town for a couple of months and was letting me sleep at his home while I looked for an apartment.

It had been years since I'd left Europe, and now I was finally back in Spain, the country where Camilla also lived and worked.

I met Camilla in a club several years ago when I was still a student. I was with a friend, and she was with one of her friends too. I approached Camilla that night and started talking to her. One of the things that impressed me about her immediately, aside from her evident and intoxicating beauty, was the fact that she informed me that she did not want to leave her friend alone and would only continue talking to me if I could find someone for her friend to talk to as well.

Although I immediately became stressed about locating my friend and convincing him to join us, I found her loyalty to her friend very moving. Luckily, I quickly found my friend and asked him to speak to Camilla's friend as a favor to me, which he did begrudgingly.

It was now several years after that meeting, which unfortunately never culminated in anything more than one date. (And that one date was cut short only an hour after we met up because Camilla had forgotten about a previous commitment and had to leave.)

Camilla had written to me that she was excited that I was back in Spain, and we were due to meet up in a club that night to go on our long-awaited second date. Camilla told me she'd be with a friend and asked if I could bring a friend too, which I did.

***

Seeing Camilla again was overwhelming, but in a pleasant way. As beautiful as she looked, nothing was more attractive than the way she spoke so softly and in such an attractive accent. I once again introduced my friend to Camilla's friend Caroline.

It was summer, and there were a lot of people at the club the four of us were in. Every time Camilla and I spoke, I wondered if this would finally be the moment when we officially became a couple. I was also very excited to surprise her with the fact that it was my birthday and that I had chosen to spend it with her.

"So, how come we never went on a second date?" Camilla asked me as both of us stood by the bar waiting for our drinks to be served.

"Because I would always see pictures of you with other guys, and I became jealous. I should have spoken to you about it, and I'm sorry. It was my mistake," I humbly responded.

Camilla smiled, but didn't respond. We continued to chat until I felt it would be a good time for me to divulge my secret.

I looked around me and saw that Caroline was by herself. I knew that if Camilla saw her friend alone, she would go over to her and stop talking to me.

"Excuse me, I'll be right back," I said to Camilla before making my way over to Caroline.

"Hey, how are you?" I asked Caroline, who did not look as happy as I was at that moment.

"I'm ok. No thanks to your friend. I think he saw some girl who was more interesting to him and left me by myself," she grumbled.

As frustrated as I was, I was not surprised.

"I'm sorry, he's like that sometimes. I say we just leave him and go somewhere else. Do you want to stay, find some other bar, or go home?" I asked.

"What about you and Camilla?" she responded.

"I'm sure Camilla would just want you to be comfortable. Besides, I am about to tell her something that hopefully will make her realize how much I like her," I admitted.

"What's that?" Caroline asked.

"It's my birthday today. She has no idea. I want her to know how much I like her," I said.

Caroline looked very surprised.

"It's your birthday, and you would go home right now if we wanted?" she questioned.

"Well, if you're uncomfortable, yes, of course! Besides, the only thing that matters to me is being around Camilla, and I don't need to be out in the city to do that!" I responded enthusiastically.

Upon hearing my response, Caroline looked at me with a strange expression, as if feeling sympathetic for me.

"I love Camilla because she's one of my best friends in the world," Caroline began, slurring her words slightly as a consequence of all the drinks she'd had that night, "but I think there's something you should know."

"What is it?"

Caroline seemed reluctant, yet equally determined to say something more.

"Is it about Camilla?" I asked, worried that there was something I'd missed in my plan to surprise her and make her realize how attracted to her I was.

Caroline nodded.

"What is it?" I inquired anxiously.

"She has a boyfriend. She's been seeing someone for a couple of years now. I'm very sorry. I thought she had told you," whispered Caroline.

First I felt as though Caroline was wrong and was saying things that weren't true due to all the drinks she'd had, but then I realized that didn't make sense. It didn't take long for me to understand that Caroline's confession finally provided me with the answers I was searching for when I wondered why Camilla never responded to any of my messages and always ran away from me whenever she got a phone call from home.

Many thoughts ran through my head, mainly regarding how I could make Camilla immediately end the relationship with whoever she was with and choose to be with me instead.

"You're a great guy. I just think you deserve to be happy," Caroline said.

I sheepishly walked back to Camilla and confronted her about what I'd just learned. Camilla said it was true, seemingly without any remorse. It made me angry that she didn't seem to understand how I could be upset over this obviously devastating revelation. However, it was at that moment that I decided to see things from a different and healthier perspective, one which I still carry to this day.

"What do you feel?" Camilla asked.

Even though this unexpected realization hurt me, I smiled. For a brief moment after Caroline informed me of Camilla's boyfriend, I had contemplated spending my time with Camilla trying to convince her to leave who she was with and be with me. However, I suddenly decided to do something different.

"I've been trying to be with you for many years. I canceled spending my birthday with my family and friends to see you. I need to start loving myself more," I announced.

Camilla's blue eyes widened, and she looked at me as if impressed.

"I'm so sorry. You're right. The truth is I'm not happy; I don't think he deserves me!" Camilla quickly added, edging slightly closer to me.

"Well, I'm not sure you deserve me," I replied before turning around and leaving. I stopped for a second to say goodbye to Caroline, who was smiling as if impressed, and then exited the club.

After that night, Camilla continued to write me and insist that we speak, but I refused. I had finally learned to love the one person I had been disregarding for many years—myself.

CHAPTER 4

FIVE STORIES ABOUT LOSS

ALEXANDER

I remember the day I arrived at school and could immediately tell that something was different. I was very young—I'm not sure exactly how young, but everyone in the classroom was still at the age where we'd sit in a semicircle around the teacher to listen to her read a story before being released to play at recess.

Furthermore, I was at the age where you are friends with whoever is nearby and wants to participate in the game or activity you are engaged in that day. There was no one I would call my best friend, and if I had been pressed to answer who I considered my closest friend, it definitely would not have been Alexander.

There was nothing bad about Alexander that would deem him unfit to be a good friend; we just never happened to be playing the same game or share any of the same interests at the same time.

I knew who he was, of course. He was the nerdy-looking boy with the bowl haircut and glasses. He always seemed to wear the same green and blue sweater and a radiant smile that never waned, except for that day in the principal's office.

As a young child, when you are asked to go to the principal's office, you immediately assume you'll be reprimanded even if you cannot recall doing anything wrong. Then again, with most of the things you do wrong as a kid, you only learn they are wrong after the fact.

I walked in somewhat sheepishly and fearfully, but was immediately relieved when I saw Alexander sitting inside with his mother and a couple more adults. I didn't know who they were, but they worked at the school. Although I was not friendly with Alexander, there was no denying that his positive energy was infectious. However, when I walked up to say hi to Alexander, I noticed his smile was not as bright as usual.

Alexander was not the only one who seemed to be troubled by something. The adults had very grave expressions on their faces, which once again made me worry that I was unknowingly guilty of some terrible crime.

The principal began speaking but struggled to get the words out as she became visibly upset. She explained that the plane bringing Alexander's father back home from a business trip had crashed and that there were no survivors.

Everyone except Alexander and I began crying. If it hadn't been for Alexander remaining stoic and seemingly unaffected by the news, I would have felt guilty for not sharing in their grief—but when you are that young, you cannot comprehend the implications and emotional considerations of such a tragedy.

After the adults managed to compose themselves, the principal explained that I was the designated support person for Alexander during what remained of the academic year. I looked at Alexander, surprised, considering I couldn't remember ever having played or conversed with him.

Alexander smiled at me, and I smiled back. I was unsure how to react, so I put my hand on his, making the adults even more teary-eyed.

The principal explained that I was deemed the best person in the class to be around Alexander and keep him company during this challenging time.

Before the meeting concluded, Alexander was given a chance to speak. At first, he spoke very pragmatically and stoically about what had happened, but when he mentioned how he knew his father would always be with him in spirit, he burst out crying harder than any of the adults.

When I got home, I told my parents about what had happened. My father surmised that they must have chosen me because I was doing so well academically.

I remember spending time with Alexander after that. He wanted to talk more than anything about his father and what he remembered about him.

Unfortunately, not too long after the accident, my mother was due to give birth to my little brother. Since we were living in a foreign country where she did not speak the local language, she opted to fly back to our home country for a few months to give birth surrounded by her extended family inside a hospital where she could communicate with the doctors.

The day I left school to fly back to our home country, I remember Alexander looking at me, confused. I was also confused; I had no idea when I would return to that school, if ever.

I was enrolled in a public school during the 12 months that we lived in my home country and I hated every second of it. I rejoiced when we finally moved back to the country where we'd been living and I could return to my old school.

I remember walking back to my old school full of doubt, wondering if people would remember me or like the fact that I was back.

The first person to greet me was Alexander, who ran over to me with open arms and a radiant smile. From that moment on, we were best friends. We were even best men at each other's weddings.

Unfortunately, after that I became immersed in work, which was very demanding. Alexander and I lived in different countries, but I always did my best to stay in touch.

When I was told by a mutual friend that Alexander had been diagnosed with a terminal illness, I could not believe that he'd been sick for months and I hadn't found out until that point. I quickly hopped on a plane to be with Alexander and stayed until he passed away almost a year later.

One of our last conversations involved a lot of apologizing from my side, first for leaving the country for my brother's birth during our childhood, and second for not having been a better friend the last couple of years.

Alexander smiled. "Do you know why you were selected to be my support person when my father died?"

"No," I responded.

"Because of your kindness. Whenever I asked you about the toys you were playing with, you would just give them to me and let me play with them. You also always answered my questions whenever I couldn't do a difficult math problem."

Alexander put his hand on mine. "Because of your kind heart, I knew you would come back now—just like I knew you would come back then."

After losing Alexander, I slowed down everything at work and learned to focus on what matters. Although he passed on, Alexander always remains with me in spirit, just like his father always remained with him.

The Green Handkerchief

Orlando had not planned on his son Daniel being sick and unable to attend school on the day of his important interview. Before finding out about his seven-year-old son's unfortunate illness he had had a very productive morning, which instilled an advantageous sense of confidence in him that he hoped would stay until he'd completed the interview that he'd spent weeks preparing for.

Since quitting his previous job, Orlando had been going through a rough time. He had not been able to secure as many interviews as he originally believed he would, and the few he'd had did not culminate in a job offer.

However, he was sure his luck was turning around now that he had had a personal friend vouch for him with the head of HR for a huge multinational company. They had a vacant position that Orlando knew he'd be perfect for.

"Are we almost at Grandma's?" Daniel asked from the backseat.

Orlando hadn't accounted for having to drive his son to his mother-in-law's place, so he was already feeling stressed and increasingly worried every time he looked at his watch. Luckily, the traffic was light, and he thought he could get to the interview just in time if everything went according to the plan he'd hastily devised after getting a call from the school.

Things would have been significantly easier if Daniel had stayed at school instead of being sent to the school nurse's office, where the nurse had taken his temperature and called Orlando to pick him up, or if Orlando's wife had been at home instead of at a doctor's appointment.

"About seven minutes away, Danny!" Orlando bellowed. He wasn't particularly fond of seeing his mother-in-law, yet he drove as fast as possible to get there.

Orlando glanced back at his son and wasn't surprised when he saw him playing with the green handkerchief. Ever since Daniel discovered the green handkerchief that Orlando sometimes wore with his black suit, he had been carrying it around with him and twiddling it between his thumb and index finger as if it were the most exciting toy he had ever gotten.

In fact, Daniel was so enamored with the handkerchief that Orlando was worried that this was symbolic of some sort of emotional problem his son might be having. Still, he was informed by a professional that there was nothing to worry about. When Orlando and his wife asked Daniel about the handkerchief, he responded with, "It makes me feel calm. I need it by my side."

Although quite stressed, Orlando smiled as he saw how much peace that green handkerchief brought his son.

Once Orlando arrived, he raced out of the car so fast he nearly fell and hit the pavement, which would have been bad considering he was wearing his lucky white shirt and didn't have time to run home and change if it got dirty.

Orlando helped his son out of the car, rang the doorbell once, and restrained himself from jabbing the bell repeatedly until his mother-in-law opened the door.

Of course! Orlando thought to himself as he surveyed the house and tried to peer through the windows to see what was taking his mother-in-law so long to come to the door.

"Is she not home?" Danny asked.

"She said she would be!" Orlando replied as he rang the doorbell a second time.

After about five excruciatingly long minutes, the door finally opened. Orlando's mother-in-law smiled when she saw little Danny and not so much when she saw Orlando.

With someone to watch over his sick child, Orlando raced back to the car and drove as fast as he could to the interview.

Luckily, he made it there with just five minutes to spare.

Orlando sat down in the waiting room and tried to slow his breathing.

"Can I get you something to drink?" the receptionist asked him, probably noticing his discomposure.

"Yes, please," Orlando replied, taking a deep and calming breath.

The receptionist came back with a paper cup filled with ice-cold water.

Orlando smiled and took a generous swig.

His throat was so dry that he coughed up the cold water and spilled an embarrassing amount all over his white shirt.

Orlando looked around, but the receptionist didn't notice until she hung up the phone and notified him that they were ready to see him.

"Oh no. Do you want to go to the bathroom first?" she asked.

"No, I'm ok, thanks!" Orlando replied foolishly as he buttoned his blazer, hoping it would cover the wet spot. Unfortunately, it didn't hide the spot at all.

"How did it go?" Danny asked as he looked down at his handkerchief.

If anyone else had asked, Orlando would have ignored the question to avoid his bad temper getting the better of him.

"Not as good as I was hoping," Orlando replied, omitting the part about everyone immediately noticing the giant wet patch on his chest when he entered the interview room.

"Why not? Didn't you have your lucky shirt?" Danny queried.

"I did. It turns out it's not as lucky as I thought…" muttered Orlando.

"Maybe you need a lucky handkerchief like me!" Danny suggested as he held up the green handkerchief a little too close to the open window.

"NOOO!" Danny wailed as the wind pulled the handkerchief out of his hand.

"What happened?" barked Orlando.

"My handkerchief just flew out the window. We have to stop!" sobbed Danny.

"We can't stop, Danny. I need to get home and change."

"Please… you have to turn around,"begged Danny.

"NO! Sit down!" Orlando exclaimed, his temper finally getting the best of him.

***

Once the sun went down and the house was quiet, Orlando was inundated with guilt. He began to see how unfair he had been to his son and wished he would have reacted better.

Orlando walked up to his son's bedroom and stood by the door for a few minutes, unsure how to apologize or explain why he had been in such a bad mood when driving home.

Instead, he decided to search for the handkerchief.

It was late and traffic was heavy, but Orlando stood on the sidewalk, looking as hard as he could for something green. He walked through the edge of the forest by the side of the road until leaves and twigs stuck to his socks and pants.

After thirty minutes of wandering through the road where his son had lost his handkerchief, Orlando decided to go home empty-handed and simply apologize.

When he got back, his wife Emma immediately greeted him.

"You need to see this," she said the second Orlando walked through the door. She guided him to Danny's bedroom and opened the door.

Danny was sitting on the floor holding Orlando's lucky white shirt and playing with it precisely as he had played with the handkerchief.

"What are you doing with my shirt, buddy?" said Orlando.

"It's just like my handkerchief," Danny replied excitedly.

"It is?" Orlando asked, confused.

"Yes, it is!" Danny replied as he held the shirt up to his face and smelled it. "It smells just like you. The handkerchief did too!"

"You liked the handkerchief because of the smell?" repeated Orlando.

"Yes, your smell makes me feel like you are next to me," Danny replied.

Orlando walked into the room and knelt by his son's side before embracing him and apologizing for what had happened earlier.

"It's ok. The water didn't ruin the smell..." Danny told his father happily. "Can I keep it?"

"Of course. Now it's *our* lucky shirt." Orlando smiled.

EMILIA

David thought about other ways of getting the money he needed without selling his favorite guitar, but couldn't think of anything.

As much as he wanted to ask for his girlfriend's advice about what to do, he was reluctant to do so because he believed she would probably be the first to encourage him to sell the instrument. In the early stages of their courtship, Anna loved hearing David serenade her and exclaimed over his talent.

However, as the years passed, she would grumble about the noise late at night and complain about the time he spent practicing instead of with her.

David had been fired from his job and struggled to make ends meet. His guitar, which he called "Emilia," had been a gift from his parents before they passed away. It had cost about half a year's salary at his old job.

Reluctantly, he posted his guitar for sale online at a price so high he hoped no one would be able to afford it. Unfortunately, only 24 hours after posting the ad, someone offered to buy it for the listed price.

David initially ignored the offer and proceeded to play Emilia all day instead of looking for a job, as he had intended.

When Anna asked why he was playing even more than usual, David replied defensively.

"Don't worry about it; soon, you won't have to hear me play anymore because I'm selling Emilia to someone next week," he snapped.

"Yeah, right," Anna scoffed. "There's no need to get aggressive with me. I'm just saying that you haven't been able to focus on looking for a job because all you do is play guitar. You aren't going to find anything if you don't devote the same energy to getting an interview."

"I'm serious. I need the money, and this is the best way to get it," David muttered.

Anna looked at her boyfriend incredulously.

After a few more attempts to find out if he was serious, Anna went from annoyed to shocked.

"I told you that my parents are willing to help you if you ask them to. You don't need to be so proud; you know that they love you," Anna said.

"It's not pride; I just don't want the relationship to become uncomfortable because I owe them money. Besides, they hate me," rebuffed David.

"You know that's not true!" insisted Anna.

"They do. If I asked them for help, they would just say no because it's me who's asking."

This was not the first time Anna and David had argued about money. The discussion ended the same way it always did, except this time Anna expressed sympathy for how David must be feeling about giving up his guitar—something he sometimes appeared to appreciate even more than his own girlfriend.

"Now all my attention can go back to you," David said.

"The attention shouldn't be on me, and you know that," argued Anna.

The following day, just as David was about to contact the buyer, he noticed that someone else had also made an offer for the guitar. This person lived in the same city, which meant that David would not need to spend any money on shipping.

David contacted the second buyer, who was very keen on buying the guitar. This comforted David because it made him feel that at least this person understood the value of the guitar and would treat Emilia with reverence.

It was tough to make the deal, but David agreed to meet the buyer by the train station near his home the next day to complete the transaction.

"It's a done deal," David informed Anna, who seemed to be significantly less shocked about David's decision today.

"I know how much the guitar means to you, but perhaps this really is the right thing to do," she told him.

David didn't answer. Whenever he thought about how much his girlfriend must revel in this sudden turn of events, he became too frustrated to even speak to her.

The next morning, David got up early and headed to the train station with Emilia safely in her hard case. If he wouldn't have felt so silly doing so, he would have cried the entire walk from the apartment to the station.

The buyer, a tall, bald businessman, was already waiting by the station with a big smile on his face. That infuriated David, who was considering making a run for it at the last minute before handing over the guitar.

The interaction was short but definitely could have been sweeter. David sat on a wooden bench by the station next to the businessman and the guitar, which he held very tightly. The transaction was immediate, and when David handed over the guitar, he felt an immense sorrow that he carried with him all the way home. He fell into bed and napped the rest of the day.

As the days passed, David became obsessed with the idea of one day making enough money to seek out the guitar he had sold and purchase it again. He knew that the more time that passed, the more the guitar would be worth, which made him work even harder to find a well-paying job.

After a couple of months of focused determination, David finally got a job that allowed him to declare himself on the road to getting his guitar back.

Anna had never seen David so happy. He got home from work every day excited to be doing something with his life.

One evening, as David entered the apartment after work, he noticed a long, rectangular cardboard box in the middle of the hallway. As soon as he closed the door behind him, Anna ran to greet him with an excited smile that was clearly about the box.

"This is for you; open it!" Anna exclaimed.

David did not hesitate to do as he was told. It did not take long for him to recognize the guitar case inside the box. David shot Anna a look of disbelief.

After ripping the box open and unzipping the guitar case, he reunited with the guitar he had been forced to sell.

"How did you find Emilia?" David asked.

"I didn't have to look for it. It's always been at my parents' place," said Anna.

"Your parents' place?" David repeated incredulously.

"My dad offered to buy it and hold onto it to protect you from yourself and your desire to sell it. He knew once you got a job, you would regret selling it, so he's been holding on to it this entire time," explained Anna.

David was speechless.

"The man who bought it from you is just a friend of his. You can't say that they hate you anymore, because they did this just to protect something you enjoy, s"he continued.

David ran to Anna, and they embraced tightly.

"So, your old man does like me, huh?" he murmured.

"Yeah, but you still need to pay him back for the guitar…" Anna replied.

CHOCOLATE-COVERED RAISINS

The first thing I noticed about my new school was that everything was made of brick and smelled like paint. To my great dismay, I'd had to leave my old school in Poland, where my family was living, to return to my home country of Colombia. Although I was technically Colombian because that's where I was born and my parents were from, I hadn't been back since we moved to Poland when I was four.

Every day I went to my new public school, I kept reminding myself that this change was only temporary and that I would be back in Poland in no time. We had returned to Colombia because my mother was pregnant with my little brother and was reluctant to give birth in Poland due to her inability to speak the language.

At first, I was excited about wearing a uniform to school, even if it was a dreary shade of mossy green. However, like almost everything else in that school, I grew tired of it fairly quickly.

Every day after school, I would come home and feel like the only one struggling with the new living situation. My mother was very happy to be reunited with her sisters and brothers, but I missed my old school where I could speak English and not be forced to speak Spanish— even though Spanish, in theory, was my native tongue. Still, I had no previous experience speaking the language for longer than five minutes at home.

One of the few aspects of this new school I preferred to my school back in Poland was that there was a mini market within the school grounds that you could access after exiting any classroom, since it was in the center of the building.

For the first couple of weeks, I didn't buy anything because even the snacks seemed so foreign to me that I was nervous about using the little money I had on foods I might not like. After a month of being the only one not snacking on something during recess, carefully observing what everyone was eating, and being given a taste of a few different snacks, I decided the chocolate-covered raisins were worth the investment.

I couldn't remember who was the one who had let me try quite a few raisins from his bag, but whoever it was had been right when they assured me that I would immediately fall in love with them.

After purchasing my first bag of chocolate-covered raisins, I was hooked. In a strange way, having a clearly defined snack for your recess purchase was a way for people to identify you among the vast amount of uniformed children.

One Friday, I was sitting on the brick floor with my classmates during recess. As I munched down on some raisins, a particularly boisterous boy named Carlos, who I had been consciously avoiding because of how different he seemed, approached me.

"Are those the chocolate-covered raisins?" he inquired as if he had found an oasis in the middle of the desert.

For a brief moment, I feared that perhaps I was not allowed to have the same snacks he ate on a regular basis, but then I realized how absurd that sounded.

"Yes," I admitted.

"They're so good, aren't they?" he enthused.

"Yeah!" I agreed.

"Can I have some?" he asked.

"Sure," I replied, handing him the packet and watching him take a generous handful.

"Thanks!" Carlos thanked me without even looking at me.

Carlos kept asking me to give him some chocolate-covered raisins for the rest of the day.

The first couple of times, I said yes, but then I decided to stand my ground and tell him no.

"What do you mean, no?" Carlos asked, interrupting the teacher—who was in the middle of reading from her textbook to the class.

"I have barely any left now. Buy your own!" I told him.

Carlos then tried to snatch the bag from my hand, but I pulled it away from him, which caused the teacher to scream at both of us.

***

After that day, Carlos and I never spoke again. We would avoid walking past each other or sitting next to each other in class or during lunch break. Things continued like this until it was finally time for my family and me to return to Poland with my little brother.

The incident with Carlos that day had caused me to miss Poland a lot, and I could not wait to leave this school, regardless of how good their chocolate-covered raisins were—which I'd stopped having altogether ever since Carlos tried to snatch my bag from me in class.

On the last day, I was waving goodbye to everyone in my class as my dad waited for me outside the school, ready to take me home, when Carlos walked up to me and handed me a folded note.

"I'm sorry," he said before walking back into the classroom.

Unsure of what was happening, I opened the letter and read the following:

> I'm sorry for what happened. My sister loves chocolate-covered raisins, and I used to bring her a bag every afternoon after school. My dad recently got fired from his job and hasn't been able to give me money for snacks. I didn't want to disappoint my sister, and I was too embarrassed to explain why I couldn't buy them for myself

anymore. I hope you understand, and I am sorry.

My dad looked at me with concern. He got out of his car, walked up to me, and put his hand on my shoulder.

"Is everything ok?" he asked.

"Yes, I just need to do something first," I replied as I stuffed the note in my pocket and ran to the snack area to buy as many chocolate-covered raisins as my lunch money would allow.

THE WRITING COMPETITION

Sarah had never been to an event like this one before. Or if she had, it had been as someone else's guest as opposed to a prize nominee.

After about a year of laborious work, she had finally finished the third draft of her novel and felt it was worthy of sending out to various writing competitions around the country.

However, she was filled with doubt. This was her first time trying to make it as a writer, and she was competing with other writers who had already published books and won previous competitions.

Sarah was proud of the book she had written, but had been assured by her family and friends that she shouldn't get her hopes up too high considering this was her first outing as a novelist. She had written a romance novel based around a tempestuous and troubled relationship she had had with her latest boyfriend, who she had broken up with a couple of years ago.

Unsure about how to cope with the end of a toxic relationship that still meant a lot to her, Sarah wrote a fictional story based on her experience with her ex-boyfriend Luke.

She struggled most with the ending of the story. In real life, she was still suffering a lot over Luke and constantly debated whether she should reach out to him and see if they could make it work this time, or finally allow herself to have a healthy relationship with someone who treated her better.

As much as she wanted to write a happy ending for her novel, she found it hard to do considering the emotional space she was in when writing the story. Therefore, she chose to end her romance with the lead female character living the rest of her days alone and saddened by the loss of the person she loved most.

The few people that Sarah showed her manuscript to said they enjoyed the book but felt the ending needed work. For the most part, Sarah agreed and didn't argue that her ending was inconclusive and somewhat tragic.

"How can I write an ending to a story I am still living? If I do that, I'll have to wait until I marry the right person, and finding them could take years," Sarah would always argue.

Regardless of her concerns about the ending, Sarah valiantly sent her manuscript to as many competitions as possible. After a month of waiting, she was finally nominated as a finalist and invited to an awards ceremony.

As Sarah walked around the event hall's reception area, she looked around the room and wondered which people around her were competitors and which were the staff.

Her friend Scarlett was next to her the whole time, looking at everyone disapprovingly.

"Everybody here looks so pretentious!" Scarlett exclaimed, speaking a little too loudly for Sarah's liking.

"Don't say that so loudly; someone will hear you!" shushed Sarah.

"Why would you want to work with people like this?" asked Scarlett.

"I wouldn't be working with them. Do you not know what a novelist is?" hissed Sarah.

Before Scarlett could respond, she became transfixed by someone walking past her.

"I wouldn't mind working with him!" Scarlett exclaimed—once again speaking a little too loudly.

Sarah turned and saw the man Scarlett was referring to. A tall, dark-haired man wearing a white T-shirt and jeans passed by and disappeared into the crowd.

The man was very handsome, which made Sarah worry that Scarlett would continue to attract attention to them by flirting outrageously.

Scarlett kept making jokes that made Sarah uncomfortable, prompting her to pull Scarlett forcibly along to find the open bar the event invitation had promised.

***

Once both women were seated in the auditorium, Sarah realized she was more nervous than she had anticipated. The stage was much larger than she had imagined it would be. As the minutes passed, more and more people filled the auditorium until there were no empty seats left.

"I can't believe so many people are here," Scarlett said as she looked around in amazement.

"I know. I can't imagine getting up on that podium if I win," Sarah admitted.

"Do you have a speech prepared?" whispered Scarlett.

Sarah turned white as she realized she hadn't even considered preparing a speech. At this point, regardless of how much hard work she had put into the manuscript, she was still determining if she even wanted to win and face such an enormous audience without a speech prepared.

As the night progressed, Sarah became increasingly nervous and almost suggested they should leave when her category was announced.

Sarah and Scarlett held each other's hands so tightly that their arms began to feel numb.

"I should have prepared a speech. What if I win?!" moaned Sarah worriedly.

Scarlett was too nervous to reply; it was apparent that despite her jokes regarding the people present at the event, she genuinely wanted her best friend to win—with or without a speech prepared.

***

"Come on, what better way to celebrate your loss than to have a drink with me and everyone else from the event? Maybe we'll meet a cute guy!" Scarlett implored.

"No one celebrates a loss!" Sarah responded as she put on her coat and tried to remember where to find the subway station that would get the two of them back to the hotel.

"Of course you do. You didn't even have a speech prepared. If you would've won, that would've been pretty embarrassing for me to watch!" countered Scarlett.

Sarah smiled and eventually consented to her friend's request.

Once they arrived at the bar, they sat down at a table by themselves and ordered drinks.

Sarah and Scarlett talked about the event and how the competition had made a big mistake by not giving Sarah the prize she deserved.

As Sarah got up from the table to head to the bathroom, she saw the handsome man from earlier. Sarah pretended not to feel overwhelmed by his presence, but failed as he approached her and stood inches away from her nose.

"I remember you. I wanted to talk to you after the event, but you left so quickly," the man said.

"Excuse me?" she stammered.

"I'm Luke."

Sarah didn't know how to react. She couldn't believe what was happening or that the handsome stranger shared the same name as her ex-boyfriend, who was also the basis for her manuscript.

Scarlett watched in awe as her friend talked to the attractive man.

Sarah returned to sit with her friend, utterly oblivious that she had never actually made it to the bathroom.

"What was that?!" Scarlett inquired.

"I have a date later tonight..." Sarah replied, still visibly shocked.

***

The date with Luke went better than Sarah ever expected. She called Scarlett as soon as she left the restaurant to give her all the juicy details.

Once Sarah arrived at the hotel, Scarlett had Sarah rehash her date over and over until it got so late that Scarlett fell asleep on the hotel room sofa.

Sarah sat down with her laptop and opened the third draft of her manuscript. She scrolled down to the end, where the main protagonist resigned herself to a life of sadness and depression after having lost the man she loved.

With a confident smile, Sarah deleted the last five pages of the document—finally ready to create a new, and hopefully better, ending to her story.

Chapter 5

Five Stories About Childhood

Two Large Dogs

Cole had always been obsessed with his childhood. He thought about it so much that he began to wonder if other people did the same. However, every time he brought it up with his friends, everyone would assert that they did not have the same relationship with their childhood that Cole did.

Perhaps the reason for this strange dynamic was that Cole still very much felt like the immature boy he had been before landing his very high-paying job and getting married. In fact, Cole felt like he was finally living the life he had envisioned for himself back when he was young. Cole had achieved everything he had ever wanted to achieve, except for getting rid of his stutter.

Cole had had a stutter for as long as he could remember. Whenever he went to stuttering support groups, he would listen to other people with a stutter talk about the age they began to stutter or even the exact moment they stuttered for the first time. Cole had never been able to speak so specifically about the origin of his stuttering, which bothered him.

It had occurred to Cole that perhaps the reason why he hadn't been able to get rid of his stutter, despite his immense success as a businessman and as a husband, was that he had no idea how his stutter had originated. Maybe finding out the source of his speech impediment would not rid him of it completely, but it might help him talk more fluently.

Cole had recently even started going to a speech therapist. During their fourth session, two things happened that made it a day he would never forget. The first thing that happened was a breakthrough when he and his therapist were talking about Cole's obsession with his childhood.

"Maybe you want to be a child again because there is something in your past that you have forgotten but need to remember," Anna, Cole's therapist, suggested. She adjusted her gold-rimmed, round glasses that were nestled between a freckled nose and two striking, blue eyes.

"Like what?" Cole asked.

"What is the earliest memory you have of when you were a child?" Anna probed.

Cole and Anna began tracing key moments in Cole's childhood until they finally arrived at a memory that Cole had completely forgotten about up until that moment.

"When I was a child," Cole began, "I couldn't have been any older than four. I was left alone in the bedroom of my parents' friend's summer villa. It was a particularly rainy night, and I woke up and went looking for my mom and dad. I jumped out of bed and ran outside into the rain, hoping to see them there. I was standing outside in the garden by a large swimming pool with fluorescent lights. Before I could make my way inside the house again, two very large, angry dogs appeared out of nowhere and began circling me and barking at me."

"Then what happened?" prompted Anna.

"I was too scared to move, so I just collapsed on the ground and started crying. That continued for a very long time until finally someone heard me and took me inside away from the dogs and dried me," remembered Cole.

Anna and Cole continued talking about the incident, and it became clear that that might have been one of the earliest causes of Cole's stutter.

The second thing that he'd never forget occurred after he got home that day. Upon arriving home, he found his wife crying by herself on the kitchen table with a half-empty bottle of red wine by her side. It did not take long for Cole's wife to confess that she wanted to move out and get a divorce.

The divorce hit Cole so hard that he stopped going to work, eventually leading to him being fired from his job.

Cole went from being at the height of success to being at his lowest point in under a year, and the worst part was that he could not understand how something like that could have happened. The more he thought about it, the more anxious he became, so at a certain point, Cole decided to stop trying to fix what was broken and simply accept things.

Cole began to obsess over returning to his childhood more than ever before. As the weeks passed and Cole began to recognize the reflection in the mirror less and less, he began to wish more than anything that he could go back to the carefree life of a child.

After finishing an entire bottle of wine by himself one night, Cole fell asleep on his black leather sofa. He had a nightmare about the night the two large, angry dogs had ambushed him. The memory felt so real that Cole woke up with a jolt and nearly fell off the sofa onto a half-finished bag of potato chips.

After regaining his composure, Cole stood up and turned on all the lights in his apartment. He then walked over to the window and gazed at the city below him. It was raining furiously, just like it had been that night in his childhood.

Even through the violent rain, Cole could hear dogs barking below him, and the noise made his skin crawl. Cole looked out the window for a long time until a thought occurred to him. Perhaps this was a way to go back to his childhood and fix things. Cole thought about how the last time he had felt this scared and alone was when the two large dogs were circling him. Maybe there was no need to go back in time because life always finds a way to present you with similar situations from the past, with the hope that you will learn how to face them as you grow older.

Cole tried to give a name to the fears that were crippling him daily. He was scared that he would never find love again, and he was scared that he had just lost the best job he would ever have. Once Cole could give his fears a name, he immediately recognized them as manifestations of the two dogs that had terrorized him as a child.

I don't need to stay paralyzed with fear this time, Cole reasoned.

Cole ran to the bathroom to shave and shower, then combed his hair and neatly tucked in his shirt.

Once he was dressed, Cole picked up all the trash from his apartment and put it into a large trash bag to take downstairs. The apartment needed a lot of work to become presentable again, so Cole decided to brave the rain and make his way out into the street in search of cleaning products.

Although the rain was falling hard, Cole did not fall to his knees and cry like he did the last time two large and scary dogs surrounded him. This time, Cole kept moving forward and has been doing so ever since.

Cole never did get rid of his stutter completely, but another thing he never did again was give up in the face of adversity. The more he worked on facing the proverbial dogs that come barking during the hard times in everyone's lives, the more fluent his speech became—to the point that he would often forget he even had a stutter.

COURAGE

Rodrigo had had a crush on the British girl next door ever since he'd first laid eyes on her. Rodrigo was too young to have a girlfriend. Still, the moment the new family moved into the empty house next door and Rodrigo's family made their way over to welcome them into the neighborhood, Rodrigo was smitten by the blonde girl with blue eyes and brown freckles.

"What do girls like?" Rodrigo would ask his older brother Sebastian, who was already in high school and therefore had a lot more experience with girls than he did.

"They like boys to be brave. If you can be brave in front of a girl, they will like you," Sebastian told him.

"What else?" Rodrigo asked.

"They like athletic boys. Boys who can run fast," shared Sebastian.

Rodrigo pondered what his brother had told him all day and the next day too.

During school, Rodrigo thought about the things that scared him most in the world.

Dogs, Rodrigo thought. Luckily, no one in the neighborhood owned any dogs, and even if they did, Rodrigo knew he would not have the courage to face a dog just to prove himself in front of the British girl.

At one point during school, Rodrigo realized he did not even know the girl's name. As soon as he arrived home, he asked his mother, who smiled and asked him why he wanted to know.

"Just curious," Rodrigo replied, which made his mother smile even more.

"Emma," she shared.

"Ok, thank you!" Rodrigo exclaimed less than a second before disappearing from the kitchen. Rodrigo ran up to his older brother's room and continued to ask him for advice about what girls liked.

After getting all the information he needed, Rodrigo returned to the kitchen, where his mother had just gotten off the phone.

"Guess what?" she asked. "We've been invited to have dinner at Emma's house tomorrow. Would you like to come?"

"Yes!" Rodrigo replied as he punched the air triumphantly.

***

Rodrigo's nerves were getting the better of him. He was sitting on the floor of Emma's room directly in front of her, and he could not think of anything to say.

"Are you scared of dogs?" Rodrigo asked.

Emma nodded enthusiastically.

"What scares you about them?" he wondered.

"I'm scared because they are fast, and they can chase me…" Emma replied.

Despite wholeheartedly agreeing with Emma and beginning to feel a little bit nervous just even thinking about the prospect of a dog chasing him, Rodrigo tried to seem calm and collected.

"I guess that might be scary…" he replied.

The door to Emma's room opened, which made Rodrigo jolt a little in fear as he had not managed to shake the thought of a dog chasing him completely out of his mind yet.

"Would you two like to go outside and play? I think some of the neighborhood kids are out there too…" Emma's mother, Monica, asked.

"Yes!" Rodrigo replied, hoping that Emma had not seen him jump in fear and trying to sound as confident as he could.

As he and Emma trooped out the door, Rodrigo decided that he did not like Emma's mother. Rodrigo never hung out with the neighborhood kids because they were older than him and, therefore, more athletic and intimidating.

As he and Emma stood outside, Rodrigo devised a plan to impress Emma and avoid embarrassing himself by trying to keep up with the older neighbor kids.

"Do you want to go to the grassy area?" Rodrigo asked, to which Emma nodded in acceptance.

Rodrigo smiled and led her a couple of blocks further to a vast grassy field that seemingly never ended. Together, they walked farther than Rodrigo had intended, but he wanted to prove to Emma that he was not scared or worried about being so far from home.

As the children walked together, they talked about the things they liked. Rodrigo listened to Emma talk about her new school and what she felt about moving to a new city. Rodrigo did his best to impress Emma by talking about how he ran a lot during recess and was one of the fastest boys in his class.

"My best friend from home has a brother who is a professional basketball player," Emma said as she opened her hands wide to feel the long blades of grass on her fingertips.

"Oh," Rodrigo replied, somewhat dejected.

Emma continued to talk about the basketball player, which began to frustrate Rodrigo.

"Do you have a boyfriend?" he interrupted.

"No. Do you have a girlfriend?" she answered.

"No, not yet," Rodrigo replied.

"Do you want one?" she prodded.

"I think so…" he said hesitantly.

Thinking that this was the best opportunity to make Emma like him, Rodrigo set out to put his plan into action. Rodrigo looked around and saw nothing but the tall grass surrounding him and Emma. He stretched up on his tippy-toes to see their houses just a few yards away.

Rodrigo then turned around again and pretended to be seeing something that was not there.

"Oh no, a giant dog! It's chasing us. We have to run!" Rodrigo screamed, trying as hard as he could to sound brave and not make it obvious that there was no dog in sight and that he was only pretending.

"What?!" Emma exclaimed.

"Come on, I'll protect you!" Rodrigo said as he grabbed Emma's small hand and pulled her forward. "I will get you home. Don't worry!"

Rodrigo ran as fast as he could and as fast as Emma would allow him to. As they ran back home, Rodrigo continued to say things that he believed would impress Emma.

"When we get home, I'll stand in front of you and make sure the dog is gone!" Rodrigo screamed as loudly as he could.

Although he was doing his best to make it seem like both he and Emma were in grave peril, Rodrigo could not help but smile as he felt that his plan was working perfectly. Emma was behind him, so he couldn't see her face, but he could feel how anxiously she was grabbing his hand. Rodrigo imagined how appreciative Emma would be once they finally got home and he could victoriously tell everyone in the house that he had protected Emma from a huge and dangerous dog that was no match for his speed and athletic abilities.

"I've never seen such a big dog. It really looks angry, but I'm not scared!" Rodrigo yelled, not worried about the fact that there was no way he'd actually see the size of the dog since his gaze was focused exclusively on the path before him.

Once both kids made it from the field to the street, Rodrigo stopped running and turned around to smile at Emma and put on a brave face. Before Rodrigo could even say anything about the fact that he was ready to stand in front of the grassy field and wait for the dog to come at him, he immediately became genuinely frightened when he saw how distraught Emma was.

Emma was crying hysterically. Her face was red and tears were running down her freckled cheeks, which made her blond locks stick to her face.

"What happened?" Rodrigo asked, as if completely oblivious to the fact that he had just informed Emma that a very dangerous and large dog was chasing them.

Emma was too scared and despondent to answer; she continued running home and left Rodrigo outside by himself, looking on in bewilderment. Rodrigo saw the door open, and

Emma's mother worriedly scooped up her daughter and took her inside the house.

"Oops," Rodrigo mumbled to himself.

***

"That little girl told you she was terrified of dogs. Is that why you made up the story about the giant dog chasing you both, just to scare her?" Rodrigo's mother asked.

Rodrigo was back home, sitting at the round, wooden kitchen table with his head slouched down and both his parents giving him looks of disapproval.

Out of shame, Rodrigo had been reticent about divulging the truth behind his motives. He knew his parents would never make fun of him for failing so miserably at making a girl like him, but he still felt too embarrassed to even talk about it.

"That little girl is very upset. You had her thinking she was about to be attacked by a scary animal. Do you think that was a nice thing to do?" Roger, Rodrigo's dad, asked. He was still in his office clothes and had his hands on his hips as he lectured Rodrigo.

"I didn't mean to scare her or to make her cry," Rodrigo mumbled.

"I think it would mean a lot to that little girl if you went over to their house and apologized," his father said sternly.

"No!" Rodrigo replied.

"Why not?" Roger demanded.

Rodrigo struggled to tell the truth, but realized that if he didn't, then his parents might think he simply wanted to make Emma sad, which was not the case at all.

"I'm scared..." he said softly.

Rodrigo's reply seemed to assuage his parents' concerns.

"What scares you?" Roger asked, bending down to be at eye level with his son.

"I'm scared she hates me and that her parents hate me," whispered Rodrigo.

"I'm sure no one hates you. You just need to do what's right and apologize," Roger said firmly.

Rodrigo struggled to find a way around needing to go over and apologize, but couldn't think of one. Eventually, he acquiesced and got up from the kitchen to put on his coat.

**

With every step Rodrigo took toward Emma's house, which were not many since they were neighbors, he contemplated running back home.

Once at the house, Rodrigo struggled to look anyone in the eye due to the overwhelming shame he was carrying. The only time he mustered the courage to look up was when Emma came down the stairs to stand before him.

With all the emotions about coming over to Emma's house to apologize, Rodrigo had forgotten how pretty Emma was.

"Hi, Emma," he said quietly.

"Hi," Emma replied sheepishly.

"I wanted to apologize for what happened. I didn't mean to scare you…" Rodrigo began.

Before continuing to speak, Rodrigo looked around and saw both his and Emma's parents looking at him. Rodrigo let out a deep sigh.

"I was trying to impress you because I like you. I wanted you to think I was brave," he said in a rush.

"Ok…" Emma replied, seemingly unphased.

"That is very sweet…" Emma's mother said as she put her hand on Rodrigo's shoulder.

On the way back home, Rodrigo complained that Emma didn't seem to care about the fact that he had confessed his crush on her. Once he was back inside, Rodrigo ran upstairs to his brother's room to tell him what had just happened.

"But don't you see, little man?" Sebastian asked. "You did exactly what you wanted to do!"

"I didn't want to make Emma cry!" protested Rodrigo.

"Not that! You were brave. You were scared to go and apologize and you did! Not just that, but you told a girl you like her; that takes a lot of courage. *I* wouldn't even be brave enough to do that!" said Sebastian.

Upon hearing his older brother's words of encouragement, Rodrigo smiled.

Sebastian continued, "And I know you were also trying to prove that you are athletic, but I think the few steps you took from our house to Emma's were more impressive than your entire sprint through the grass field because those were steps of courage."

"But Emma wasn't impressed that I was brave and told her I liked her," said Rodrigo.

"That's OK, because you shouldn't do it for her. You should be brave for yourself," reassured Sebastian.

Rodrigo jumped up onto his older brother's bed and sat down next to him.

"Thank you." Rodrigo thanked Sebastian with a beaming smile. "How did you get so good at explaining things?"

Sebastian smiled back and said, "Girls also like a poet... but don't start devising any new plans."

THE HAUNTED HOUSE

Rodrigo was invited to accompany his father and mother to a work-related dinner. Roger, Rodrigo's father, was being honored by his coworkers and given an award for his many years of service to the company.

Rodrigo was indifferent about attending the event. But while sitting in the car with his parents, he heard his father say something that bothered him so much that he could not think about anything else after hearing it.

"You know something, buddy?" Roger asked as he drove everyone to the event, which was taking place in the country club of a gated community not too far from their house.

"What?" Rodrigo asked, struggling to feel comfortable in the first suit he had ever worn in his life.

"In my speech, I'm going to talk about you, so get ready to have all the spotlight," enthused Roger.

At first, Rodrigo became excited about the prospect of having a room full of people looking at him and hearing about him. However, once they arrived at the event, there were so many serious-looking grown-ups walking around that Rodrigo felt intimidated and overwhelmed.

There were also a lot of lights and loud sounds, which made Rodrigo start to feel terrified about having all the attention turned on him. Rodrigo decided to ask his father not to mention him, but his dad was busy greeting everyone in the near vicinity. Every time Rodrigo tried to speak to his dad, another person approached Robert and began congratulating him.

Before he knew it, Rodrigo was seated inside a very large auditorium with his parents. The room was so loud that it was virtually impossible for Rodrigo to speak to his father, who was not seated directly beside him.

Rodrigo saw one of his friends at the event, whose dad also worked with Robert.

"Mom, can I go play with Mitchell?" he asked.

"OK, but don't go too far!" his mom cautioned.

The idea was not to go far but to stay away from the conference room for long enough that no one would look at him, even if his father did mention Rodrigo in his speech.

***

The night was cold, and things were much more peaceful and quiet outside the auditorium.

"You know, I heard that this place has a haunted mansion. Apparently, it's not far, and if you go inside and stay long enough, you come out braver," Mitchell said as he wandered around the grounds with Rodrigo.

"Awesome. Can we see it?" Rodrigo asked.

"Sure!" Mitchell led Rodrigo a few yards away and stopped in front of what looked like an abandoned house. The walls looked like they may have originally been white but were now streaked with sooty gray, as if the building had survived a great fire.

No lights were visible inside, and the boys could tell it would not be any warmer inside than outside.

There was no denying that the building was creepy. The darkness inside seemed to be even more pronounced than the darkness outside.

"Yeah, if you ask me, that place is definitely haunted," Rodrigo asserted.

"I don't even like looking at it!" Mitchell added, quivering as he spoke—partly due to the cold, but mainly because of the haunted house.

"I bet it looks better from the inside," said an older and more confident voice behind Mitchell and Rodrigo.

Unable to contain his fear, Mitchell yelped before turning around to face a group of five older boys surrounding them, all with mischievous smiles on their faces.

"Who are you?" Rodrigo asked.

"The Harleys," Mitchell responded somewhat regrettably. "They live here."

"We don't call ourselves that, but it's not the worst name for a group. I think it has something to do with the awesome bikes we have. My name is Axl," explained the gang's tallest and most confident-looking member.

"Motorcycles?" Rodrigo asked excitedly.

"Sure. Motorcycles, why not?" Axl responded as the rest of his gang laughed. "In fact, I'll let you look at mine and have a ride on it if you go inside that house and stay there for at least five minutes."

"No way!" Mitchell responded, as if the dare was directed at him.

Rodrigo looked at the scary building.

"And like your little friend said. You don't have to worry about ever being scared again in life because once you go inside, you come out fearless," Axl said.

After a few contemplative moments, Rodrigo smiled and turned to face the Harleys.

"I'll do it!"

***

The inside was not as scary as it looked on the outside. However, Rodrigo couldn't help but think of all the scary films his older brother had made him watch a couple of years ago and how this decrepit, squalid old building would be exponentially more terrifying with some eerie background music accompanying Rodrigo's every trepid step.

There was light coming in from somewhere and loud voices in the distance, but he couldn't make out exactly where they were coming from. The more he tried to listen to the voices, the more frightened he became, so he decided to ignore them and simply make his way up to the second floor, which was the deal he had made with the Harleys.

Rodrigo made his way up a long, spiral staircase that wound past a hole-infested wall filled with oil paintings of stern-looking people. Rodrigo tried to ignore their intimidating looks as he approached the balcony.

Once he made it to the balcony, he looked down and saw Mitchell standing by himself, appearing highly distressed.

"Where are the Harleys?!" Rodrigo cried from the top of the balcony, which was nowhere near as high up as he thought it was.

"They left! And they did something to lock the door shut!" Mitchell replied anxiously.

"What?!" Rodrigo exclaimed, immediately regretting speaking so loudly—just in case his voice might wake up whatever ghosts were still slumbering inside the haunted house he was trapped in.

"I don't know what they did, but they just got on their bikes and left. Can you find a way out from inside?" called Mitchell.

Even if there was another way to exit the building from the inside, Rodrigo was not overly keen on exploring the house out of fear of discovering things that could end up haunting him more than the films his brother had inflicted upon him.

But, not wanting to sound too frightened in front of Mitchell, Rodrigo told him he'd find a way out and darted back downstairs to see if there was another door.

After a few minutes of slowly inching across the floor, Rodrigo decided to move faster.

The deeper Rodrigo went into the house, the louder the sound of people talking became, and the more light emerged from the cracks in the wall.

Suddenly, Rodrigo heard footsteps approaching him. Rodrigo's heart began to race as the footsteps got louder and continued moving toward him. A tall, human-like silhouette began to emerge from the shadows, making Rodrigo scream and run toward the thread of light emanating not too far from where he was standing.

The farther Rodrigo ran, the brighter the light became until he realized it was coming from the other side of a large door that was slightly ajar.

Rodrigo stopped in front of the door and heard the footsteps running toward him.

Almost involuntarily, Rodrigo pushed the door open and darted through. He immediately became blinded by the light, and the loud noises and voices emanating from the other side suddenly went silent.

After a couple of seconds, Rodrigo's eyes adjusted to the light enough for him to notice where he was standing. Although he was now immersed in light and surrounded by people who were definitely not ghosts, Rodrigo felt no less frightened. Then, he realized that his father was standing at a podium in front of him.

"Rodrigo?" Roger asked as he looked away from his notes and stopped speaking to his friends, family, and colleagues.

Noticing that his son could not speak, Roger turned back to his microphone and once more addressed the room full of people.

"Everyone, I want to introduce you to my son Rodrigo. The bravest boy in the world," he announced.

Roger ushered his son to come toward him and join him at the podium. Rodrigo ran to his dad as the entire room clapped.

Roger continued making his speech with his son by his side and, when he was done, they returned to the table to join Rodrigo's mother.

"So, your solution to not wanting your dad to direct people's attention to you was to run on stage in the middle of his speech?" Rodrigo's mother asked.

"It wasn't on purpose!" cried Rodrigo.

"Were you scared?" she continued.

"No," he stated.

"How come?" Roger asked.

"I guess staying inside the haunted house for five minutes does make you brave," said Rodrigo.

Although Rodrigo's parents did not understand what their son meant by that statement, they could tell by the smile on his face that he was no longer nervous. Instead, he was ready to have a lovely, relaxing evening.

AXL

Axl had just moved into our gated community and was already more popular than me. He was more athletic, better-looking, and more outgoing. However, since our mothers had been friends back when they were in grade school, Axl and I were introduced one day so that we could become friends and so I could show him around the neighborhood.

To my chagrin, Axl ended up introducing me to kids in the neighborhood I had known for several years but had never become friends with due to my introverted nature. I admired Axl for his social, charismatic personality.

One day, I invited Axl to my house. He was the first person I had ever invited over, and the fact that the most popular boy in the neighborhood would be at my place was overwhelming.

At first, we played around and had fun scaring each other and making crazy drinks from what we could find in my parent's fridge and the storage area.

During a particularly long game of hide-and-seek, where I was hiding and Axl was supposed to be trying to find me, I heard my baby brother crying frantically in his crib. This was not a particularly strange occurrence, but the way he was crying and the way he did not stop started to worry me.

I quickly ran up to his bedroom and found Axl throwing toys into the crib at him from a distance. Almost out of instinct, I screamed at Axl to leave the house, which he did immediately.

I picked up my brother and sat on the sofa next to his crib, holding him in my arms until he calmed down. I learned that day not to try and be friends with people just because they are considered popular or exciting by others.

THE BLACK SLOPES

Dana had never spent so much time with adults in his life. When his parents had invited him to join them on a ski trip with his father's work colleagues, Dana had said yes because he had always wanted to learn to ski.

It was the last day, and he was now standing at the top of the black diamond run with his father's work colleagues because Dana's parents had gotten food poisoning the night before and could not join them.

"So, Dana, last night you said you would be fine with the black diamonds. That's why we're here. Are you still sure you can hang?" Rob asked with a condescending tone.

It immediately dawned on Dana that saying yes to skiing the black diamonds had been a mistake, but he would never show fear in front of five grown men.

After nodding their heads in approval, all the men began skiing down the run with Dana right behind them.

Dana screamed every second of the way down but miraculously managed not to fall even once, even though he sometimes downright closed his eyes to avoid seeing what he believed was about to be his ultimate demise.

The four adults kept skiing around him to ensure he was fine. It was easy for them to spot Dana, since he was the only person screaming the entire way down the mountain.

Once the group made it to the bottom of the mountain, Dana collapsed in a heap on the snow.

"Dana, you were doing so good! You only fell at the last moment," called one of the men.

Dana was breathing heavily but finally managed to get himself up with the help of Rob and the others.

"I was just too exhausted from all the screaming to stay standing up!" Dana exclaimed.

Chapter 6

Five Stories About Work

The New Job

Lorena was nervous about starting a new job in Mexico. Although she was technically Mexican, she hadn't been back since she was four years old and her family moved to Europe.

Lorena had just graduated from a very prestigious university but had failed to find a job. Instead, she had spent the six months after graduation partying and socializing with her friends, despite her parents' protests.

Whenever Lorena's parents would insist that she focus on finding a job, Lorena just responded that she would do it later and that she deserved to have fun with her friends after finishing her studies.

Fearing that their daughter would not understand the responsibility she had to be independent and self-sufficient, Lorena's parents decided to cut her off financially. When Lorena failed to find a job and could no longer rely on her parents to maintain her lifestyle, she decided to accept a job her uncle was offering her back in Mexico.

Although she was nervous about flying back to Mexico by herself, she was confident that this would only be a temporary solution and that she would indubitably find a job back in Europe in a year or so.

Once she arrived at her uncle's company, she was introduced to everyone. The office was tiny, and the people working there were very unlike the people she was used to hanging out with back home. First of all, no one spoke English, and Lorena's Spanish was not that great. No one in the office, except for Lorena's uncle, had ever left Mexico. Most had not even been to college.

Lorena immediately felt out of place, which made her nervous. Even if she could speak Spanish fluently, or if her coworkers could speak English, she worried that they would prefer not to speak to her.

Whenever she walked into the office, everyone either got quiet or started whispering to each other in Spanish. Lorena had never felt ashamed of her lifestyle until moving to Mexico and working for her uncle. Everyone there seemed reluctant to engage with her because of all the countries she had lived in and all the opportunities her parents had given her to live a comfortable, privileged life.

The most popular person in the office was a younger guy called Fernando. Fernando usually talked loudly and made a lot of jokes but would become visibly more apprehensive whenever Lorena would arrive at work.

Lorena usually went out for lunch, while everyone else brought Tupperware containers filled with food. Her parents advised her to do the same, but she was worried that it would be devastatingly humiliating if she brought leftovers from home too. Still, she always ended up sitting by herself in the dining hall, away from everyone else in her office, while they all ate together.

Every day when Lorena arrived home from work, the first thing she would do was apply for jobs back in Europe—she was desperate to leave the situation she was in.

One day, Lorena was driving to work in a car that belonged to her parents. It was a Thursday and there was heavy traffic, as usual. Lorena was about twenty minutes from the office when a taxi driver cut her off a little too aggressively. Lorena did not see the taxi in time, which meant the driver had to brake very loudly and suddenly.

Lorena gasped. The braking noise had been so loud, and the cars were so near each other, that she was unsure if they had collided.

Before she could do anything, the driver got out of the taxi and began violently banging his large, greasy hands against the window of Lorena's car.

Unsure of what the angry driver was saying, Lorena just recoiled back in her seat and waited for the abuse to end, which it finally did after a very long two minutes of being screamed at.

The driver kicked Lorena's car before storming back over to his taxi and driving off.

Seeing the light in front of her turn green, Lorena had no option but to continue driving to work. Once she arrived at work and parked her car in the outdoor parking lot, she burst into tears, hands still on the steering wheel. Suddenly, every frustration she had been harboring regarding her new life rose to the surface until she was overcome by a wave of emotion.

After a couple of minutes of despondent crying, there was a knock on her window. Lorena could not see who it was before wiping the tears from her eyes. It was Fernando.

Lorena ashamedly rolled down the window.

"Are you OK?" Fernando asked. Lorena was shocked to hear him speak English, albeit with a strong accent.

"Yes, I'm fine," Lorena responded, failing miserably to compose herself.

"What happened?" queried Fernando.

Lorena explained the incident with the taxi driver, but left out the part about feeling alienated at work.

Fernando scoffed in frustration.

"The taxi drivers think they are the kings of the street. I am so sorry!" he sympathized.

After a couple of minutes, Fernando invited Lorena to grab some coffee before heading into the office. She hesitantly accepted.

Lorena finally confessed to Fernando about how she had been struggling with the move to Mexico, which made her cry again regardless of how hard she was trying to control her emotions.

"Why don't you sit with us during lunch?" Fernando asked.

"I'm scared that you don't want to talk to me..." Lorena replied, once again wiping tears from her face.

Fernando explained that the office thought she did not hang out with them because everyone else came from more humble beginnings. After half an hour, Fernando and Lorena agreed that they had both been making false assumptions about each other and decided to stop doing so.

Fernando invited Lorena to lunch with the entire team. At lunchtime, when he explained what happened with the taxi driver, everyone began defending Lorena.

"They think they can do whatever they want!" someone shouted in anger.

The next day, Lorena walked into the office and was greeted kindly by everyone. The team invited her to drinks after work, and she happily accepted.

From that moment on, Lorena learned to enjoy her work. Lorena began to work on her Spanish and helped Fernando and the others with their English.

About a month later, during a long weekend, Lorena got an email from a company back in Europe saying that they wanted to interview her for a job. After a couple of minutes spent deliberating her options, Lorena replied that she was no longer available for an interview.

After replying to that email, Lorena felt relieved and satisfied. She picked up the phone to call Fernando and invite him over for some lunch or a coffee.

Fernando told her that he would love to come but asked her to stay inside when he arrived. When Lorena asked why, he cheekily replied that he would have to take a taxi to her place and didn't want Lorena to start crying uncontrollably when she saw the taxi driver.

Lorena laughed to herself. To her surprise, she was thankful that she had almost collided with the taxi that day. If it hadn't been for that incident, she might have never found a way to connect with her coworkers, who in time became better friends to her than any other friends she had ever had.

FRIEND BOSS

Alan had been working at the same marketing agency as Tatiana for three years. Tatiana had been hired about a year after Alan and was initially supposed to report to him. However, only a couple of months after Tatiana joined the company, the CEO made some changes in the company and promoted Tatiana to become an account manager for a different client, meaning she had similar responsibilities as Alan.

Although they did not work on the same account, it did not take long for Alan and Tatiana to become best friends. They would routinely go to lunch together and hang out after work. Alan and Tatiana became such close friends that people would often gossip and speculate that they were secretly dating, which was completely untrue. Alan and Tatiana kept lecturing everyone on the importance of not making false assumptions because it could lead to conflict in the workplace, but at the end of the day, they did not care what people thought about their friendship. The truth was that they never had any intention of evolving their relationship from friendship to romance, regardless of what people said behind their backs.

Even on the most challenging days in the office, Alan and Tatiana always supported each other emotionally. They sometimes even helped with some of the work that the other person had to do.

One day, Alan was called into his boss's office along with Tatiana. This was new, since they didn't work on the same account. For a brief moment, Alan was worried that the gossip regarding their false love affair had been brought to his manager's attention and that there would be repercussions because of it.

As Alan and Tatiana sat in front of Leo, Alan's boss, Alan began to prepare how he would convince Leo that nothing was going on between him and Tatiana.

"Alan, we've lost your account. The client has decided to go look for another agency," Leo explained with a frustrated look.

As anxious as Alan was before hearing this news, now he felt even worse.

"Don't worry; you are not getting fired. Instead, you are going to join Tatiana's account. Since she is the account manager, you will be reporting directly to her. She is now your boss," continued Leo.

Alan and Tatiana looked at each other, trying to contain their laughter. As bad as this revelation was, at least Alan still had his job, and he would be able to work closely with his best friend.

However, as the weeks and months passed, the dynamic between Alan and Tatiana began to change—and not for the better. Alan started to feel reluctant to hang out with Tatiana, considering they were constantly together at work and she continuously gave him work to do. Even when it was time to have lunch, Alan was scared that Tatiana would get mad if he stopped for lunch before she was ready to take a lunch break.

Alan stopped having lunch with Tatiana altogether and would often come back down to the office to see her still working, which made him feel guilty.

After some time, the two stopped speaking to each other as friends. One night in the office, when everyone had already left and it was only Alan and Tatiana working, Alan realized just how awkward the relationship between him and Tatiana had become.

It was very late, and he needed to finish up within the hour if he wanted to catch the last bus home. There was still some work to be done, but he figured he could do it at home or early the next morning. However, considering he always left for lunch before Tatiana, he felt guilty leaving the office first, too.

Alan worked as fast as he could but kept getting distracted by the clock. If he missed the last bus, he would need to take a taxi, which would be very expensive.

"Is there somewhere you have to be?" Tatiana asked as she noticed Alan continuously looking at his watch.

"No, just hoping I manage to catch the last bus," Alan replied, trying to sound as amicable as possible.

Tatiana grunted as if someone had just handed her a lot more work to do that night.

"Just go home and get some rest. I'll finish up," she said gruffly.

"No, it's ok. I can stay…" offered Alan.

"Don't worry. If it's the last bus, you should take it," ordered Tatiana.

Alan wanted her to know that he was willing to stay, but decided it would be best for him to leave the office.

Feeling somewhat ashamed, Alan left the office and waved goodbye to Tatiana. As he closed the translucent door behind him, he heard Tatiana sigh with exasperation. He stood by the door for a minute and heard Tatiana pull out her phone and make a call.

He could not make out exactly what she was saying, but he heard enough to realize she was complaining that she was disappointed. As much as Alan wanted to hear more, he eventually had to run to catch the last bus—thankfully making it just in time.

**

The next morning, Alan walked into work and saw Tatiana in Leo's office, looking frustrated.

"Why is she in there?" Alan asked the person in the cubicle next to him.

"No idea, but she doesn't look happy…"

Alan suddenly felt angry. He had a suspicion that Tatiana was complaining to Leo about how Alan had left the office before finishing his work the night before.

Unbelievable, he thought and decided he was no longer going to worry about ever being friends with Tatiana again.

Not long after that, Alan was called into Leo's office. As Alan walked in, Tatiana left.

Alan sat down, angry that the situation between him and Tatiana had gotten to such a bad place.

"There is going to be some restructuring going on. In light of some new information given to me today, you are no longer going to be working for Tatiana…" began Leo.

Before Leo could finish his sentence, Alan abruptly—almost involuntarily—stood up from his chair in a rage. He opened the door behind him and yelled at Tatiana.

"Was it so hard to just speak to me?" Alan protested. "Now you are getting me fired?"

"What?" Tatiana asked incredulously.

"We used to be friends, and now you are making me lose my job because I leave the office minutes before I miss the last bus? That is so unfair!" snapped Alan.

"No one is losing their job," Leo exclaimed as he appeared behind Alan. "This is just a demotion."

"Why should I get demoted?" Alan protested.

"You are not getting demoted!" Leo responded.

"I am," Tatiana added.

"What?" Alan asked, confused.

"I think you two need to have a talk..." Leo suggested.

"I don't understand," Alan said as he took a sip of his coffee.

"I have just been feeling so frustrated and ashamed about how you see me as your boss and not your friend anymore. Last night I became angry at myself when I watched you almost miss your bus because of me," Tatiana responded.

"That's why you were upset last night?" asked Alan.

"Of course. I stopped joining you for lunch because I want you to relax, and I know that you can't do that around me anymore, which is why I asked Leo for a demotion," shared Tatiana.

"You asked for a demotion?!" sputtered Alan.

"Yes. I just want to be friends with you again, even if it means that I'm not the account manager anymore. Leo is going to find someone new to replace me; that is what he meant when he said this was just a demotion," explained Tatiana.

Alan was in shock. He had no idea Tatiana had been suffering so much over the loss of their friendship, or that it meant so much to her.

"I am so sorry. I completely misread the situation. I have missed you as a friend, too," Alan confessed.

Tatiana and Alan hugged and ended up staying at the café longer than they probably should have. Tatiana explained that she believed Alan hated having her as a boss and was trying to distance himself from her as much as he could.

After settling their issues, Alan convinced Tatiana that she should stay on as the account manager instead of asking to be demoted. Instead, they agreed to communicate better instead of making assumptions without asking each other for the truth.

As they walked back to the office, Tatiana laughed to herself.

"What's so funny?" Alan asked.

"You know what we can't do anymore?" she told him.

"No, what?" he replied.

"Lecture everyone about the importance of not making assumptions about people..." Tatiana replied. Alan smiled in agreement.

THE CALL CENTER

After working at the same marketing agency for over five years, Alan was finally promoted to an account manager position. His new account was a pharmaceutical client that ran a call center. Alan had never even been inside a call center, but he was excited about his new, expanded responsibility.

Alan had been waiting years to get promoted. There were several other accounts in the agency he worked in that interested him and that he felt he would be more comfortable managing than the pharmaceutical call center account he was given. However, Alan was eager to prove himself worthy of the opportunity and to learn as much as he could from the experience that awaited him.

After a quick conversation with his boss Leo, Alan assured Leo that he would improve the call center and make the account one of the most profitable for the company.

One day, Alan was tasked with visiting the call center to meet the agents he would be working with. Alan was more nervous than he had expected. The client would be there waiting for him to make the formal introductions.

When Alan arrived, he felt overwhelmed with nerves, but was determined to conceal his nervousness from the client. The client showed him around and introduced Alan to three call center agents who would be his daily points of contact.

Alan spent the entire day at the call center learning about what the job entailed. There was a lot of information to process, but Alan acted as if everything he was hearing was being retained in his memory. Unfortunately, it wasn't.

Before the day was over, Alan noticed a beautiful, young, blonde call center agent sitting on her desk taking calls and writing things down. As much as he tried to focus on the work, Alan couldn't stop looking at the gorgeous blonde.

When the day ended and Alan was preparing to follow the client out of the building, he went up to the girl he had been admiring for hours and asked for her name.

"Jess," the girl replied.

"Can I have your number?" he asked.

Jess seemed reluctant at first but eventually wrote her number on a piece of paper and handed it to Alan, who was overjoyed.

Once Alan arrived home, he sent a message to Jess and asked her out on a date. It took a couple of hours for her to reply, but Jess finally answered that she'd meet up with him.

***

"The client wants to move the call center to this building. I need you to set up these empty offices as a call center so that the new agents can come in next week and start making their calls from here," Leo informed Alan the next day.

Although Alan had no idea how to do that, he once again purposefully exuded false confidence to appear comfortable in his new position and assured Leo he would come in on Saturday and have the space ready for the call center agents before Monday.

***

It was now Friday evening, and no matter how much research Alan did, he did not feel remotely confident about setting up a call center. He hadn't informed Jess about his predicament because he was still hopeful that he would manage to finish his work on time and be able to meet her for a dinner date on Saturday evening.

After arriving home that evening and realizing that he would need the entire weekend to set up the call center, Alan begrudgingly picked up his phone to cancel his date with Jess.

However, before doing so, a thought occurred to him. Alan pondered whether asking Jess to come to the office with him on Saturday to help him would be a good or terrible idea. In terms of what he needed to accomplish at work, it made sense.

Jess had experience working in a call center and could potentially advise him on what needed to be done to set one up successfully. This way, he would not fail his first big assignment and also would be able to spend time with Jess on Saturday, even if it wasn't what would typically be considered a date.

Alan pondered the right thing to do until he realized there was no other option.

Alan called Jess and informed her of his predicament. Jess laughed and said she would be willing to help him tomorrow afternoon at the office.

"It's a date! Thank you so much!" Alan exclaimed on the phone.

"Is it?" Jess asked on the other line.

"Sort of…" Alan said tentatively.

***

Much to Alan's dismay, Jess arrived a little late to the office. Although Alan had already been there for two hours, he hadn't managed to get anything done other than pace frantically as he tried to calm his nerves.

"It's ok… don't worry. I will help you," Jess reassured him.

Alan tried to act like he knew what he was doing, but soon realized it was better to simply let Jess take control of the situation.

After about an hour, Jess had completely set up the communication lines and said that the call center was fully operational.

Alan tried it out the way Leo instructed him to do once it was finished, and everything worked the way it was supposed to.

"I owe you big time!" Alan exclaimed as he wiped the sweat from his forehead.

Jess looked at him and smiled.

"What is it?" Alan asked.

"You know, I was about to cancel our date before you called me and asked for my help..." Jess confessed.

"How come?" wondered Alan.

"When you walked into the call center, you were acting so arrogant. I was unsure if we would get along. But today, you seemed completely different, so I'm glad we met up," Jess told him.

Alan explained that he had been trying to portray the image of someone who knew what they were doing as a way to protect their job. Jess laughed.

"I get that. Maybe next time, just be more humble; there are always people willing to help people who need it," Jess suggested.

Alan nodded in agreement.

"Especially if you ask someone who is an absolute master of their craft—like me," Jess quipped as she smiled and exited the office.

THE BLOG POST

Miranda had been working as an accountant for over ten years. Although the work was somewhat monotonous and easy for her, Miranda relished the security it provided.

It was a sunny Friday afternoon. There was positive energy in the office as people prepared for the start of the weekend. All the windows were open, and a soft summer breeze and bright sunlight drifted into the office and made the few people still working even more eager to leave.

Miranda was typing away on her laptop as she answered the last few unread emails in her inbox. Once she was finished, Miranda took a sip from her translucent plastic water bottle and shut her laptop with a triumphant smile.

The sound of her laptop closing on a Friday afternoon was one of her favorite sounds in the world. Miranda looked around the office and saw that everyone was too focused on getting their work done as quickly as possible to notice that she was about to leave.

Before Miranda could take the few steps over to the coat rack to put on her green coat, she heard one of the sounds she detested most in her life: the sound of her boss's office door opening.

"Miranda, can you come into my office?" her boss Leo asked as he poked his head through the door and then disappeared back inside.

"Coming!" Miranda replied as she quietly winced and shut her eyes in dismay. This time, everyone in the office saw her and smiled sympathetically.

Miranda took another sip of water and then slammed the water bottle down on her mahogany desk a little too aggressively. As she made her way to Leo's office, she hoped that she was about to be given some great news that would make her ride home all the more pleasant.

Once the pleasantries were out of the way, Leo asked Miranda to sit—something he rarely did unless he wanted to talk about something serious.

Miranda sat down and noticed everyone outside was looking at her through the transparent glass walls of Leo's office. Even though she felt quite nervous, Miranda smiled at everyone stoically.

"We're going to have to let you go. I am so sorry," Leo said gently.

At first, Miranda was convinced she had misheard her boss, but then she saw an expression of guilt on Leo's face that she had never seen before.

"I really am sorry, but it is out of my hands. Losing the pharmaceutical account put us in a bad place, financially, that we are still scrambling to get out of. I tried my best, but I have to follow orders," Leo explained.

Miranda couldn't help but turn around to look at her coworkers through the glass wall. Once they noticed her confused and shocked expression, they stopped smiling and turned away as though they felt embarrassed for watching.

Unsure of what to do or say, Miranda began rubbing her hands along her blue jeans and making noises that she hoped would, at some point, turn into words. When nothing comprehensible came out, Leo continued explaining the situation and trying to make it seem like it was not his fault. Even though Miranda knew he was right, nothing Leo said assuaged the anxiety rising in her chest at the prospect of no longer having a job.

"I'm sorry," Leo said, his dark brown eyes locked on Miranda as if worried that she would at any moment start screaming, "but maybe you can make something positive out of this."

That night, Miranda canceled her plans as soon as she got home. She camped out in her TV room with a big plate of her favorite snacks and watched reruns of her favorite comedy show until she fell asleep on the sofa without even changing out of her work clothes.

***

It had been over a month since Miranda had been fired. She had taken a week off to relax and enjoy the freedom she had never asked for. Miranda's friends and family had reassured her that she would find a new job in no time. However, after her one-week break, Miranda had been applying to at least ten jobs every day and still was not getting any interviews.

Trying not hard not to crumble under the pressure she was feeling, Miranda went out for a walk by herself to clear her mind. During her walk, she thought about what her ex-boss had said to her, about how maybe she could "make something positive out of this."

What does that even mean? Miranda pondered, feeling frustrated.

She thought about what her younger, more rebellious self would have thought about leaving her accounting job and smiled. When Miranda was still a student, she loved to write stories. The only reason she had become an accountant instead of a writer was that she was pressured into it by her parents, who did not believe in her literary abilities.

The more Miranda thought about her situation, the more frustrated and worried she became. To ensure she didn't succumb to a panic attack, Miranda decided to go back home and figure out something that might calm her nerves.

Once she was back home, she thought about what her old writing teacher used to tell her about the best way to go about writing. She had always told Miranda, "Whenever you feel there is so much inside you that it cannot be contained, let it out onto the page."

Miranda sat by her desk and began writing her frustrations down on the white computer paper that she pulled out of the printer next to her feet. To her surprise, she did not struggle at all to write and very soon needed to pull out another five sheets of paper from the printer to keep writing down her thoughts.

Miranda continued to write every day for the next week. When she wasn't writing, she was reading what she wrote and laughing at how silly some of her ideas were. Miranda spent hours flopped on her white sofa, editing some of the things she had written to make them flow better—even though she had no plans of allowing anyone other than herself to read them.

***

Another two weeks had gone by, and Miranda had nothing to show for her job-hunting efforts other than the frustrations she kept building up and then releasing onto the page. Her bedroom was starting to look like a stationery store, what with all the pens and pieces of paper lying on the floor and the nightstand by her bed.

As much as she wanted to keep writing, Miranda felt that she needed to evolve her process in a way that would keep this new habit exciting and perhaps even conducive to her professional development somehow.

Miranda took the heavy stack of white paper to her desk and sat in front of her laptop. She once again pondered what Leo had said to her about considering being laid off as something positive.

After glancing at the pages before her and combining what Leo said with what her old writing teacher used to say, Miranda went online and found a free website where she could write blog posts.

Since she had already diligently edited all her written work, Miranda typed out the best snippets that she'd come up with during the past weeks and created a blog post to share her feelings regarding being fired and struggling to find work.

Every morning after that, Miranda would sit down and transcribe the thoughts she'd jotted down on scrap paper into a new blog post. After completing five posts, Miranda finally mustered the courage to share links to her blog posts online—asking people to read, share, and comment with their thoughts.

The next day, Miranda woke up to find she had several new emails from businesses that wanted to get in touch with her about her blog posts.

Miranda responded to the emails and discovered that more than one company wanted her to be a freelance journalist or content writer after how popular her blog posts had become shortly after they were posted.

Before deciding what path to take, Miranda once again went for a walk to clear her head. Once outside and surrounded by the verdant landscape she loved so much, she struggled to do anything other than think about whether she should accept the writing job.

Miranda removed a white, pocket-sized notebook from the pocket of her green raincoat and began to write down her thoughts to try and organize them into anything that resembled a coherent thought. Before she could even read through what she had written, she realized how simple things really were. Miranda replaced the small notebook inside her coat and sprinted home.

Once she was sitting in front of her laptop, Miranda wrote the company that interested her the most to inform them that she accepted the job offer.

It was years before Miranda ever looked inside the white notebook to see what she had written that day as she walked through the forest by her apartment trying to clear her busy mind. The day she found the notebook, she was putting all her things into boxes to finally move into a bigger house in the city as a result of her success as a full-time journalist.

Miranda sat down on the bedroom floor of the apartment that would soon belong to someone else. She smiled as she read the last thing she had written before making the best decision of her life.

The last entry read: *I am writing because I need to, and without it, I will feel lost.*

THE DONATION

Pete looked at the watercolor painting he had been working on for the past hour and winced. He contorted his neck and squinted to try and see something that disappointed him less, but to no avail.

Why do I bother? Pete asked himself as he aggressively threw the paintbrushes down on the floor and slumped over, deeply dejected. He eyed his attempt at painting a boat sailing through a storm and realized that it was nowhere near as good as he had imagined it to be in his head.

Pete had spent several weeks deciding what to do and which voice he should listen to, his own or his father's, after graduating from college. Pete had studied marketing because his father, Carl, had always wanted him to go into business like him. However, Pete was a very different person from his father. Carl was a very analytical man who never understood Pete's desire to become a painter. Although he encouraged Pete to follow his passion, he also advised him to be thoughtful about what career path he chose to pursue.

"There will always be signs that will help guide you down the right path," Carl would tell his son right after Pete received good grades in math or brochures inviting him to apply to study business at top universities.

Pete had been getting job offers to work for various marketing firms ever since leaving school, which he tried to tell himself were not actually signs that he should pursue a business career like his father. However, after being so disappointed by his first attempt at painting what was on his mind, Pete began to accept that perhaps it was time to accept that the world was clearly telling him that he was not destined to become a famous painter.

Pete started pacing frantically in his room as he tried to decide what he should do next. After a while, he opened his computer and began responding to the emails he had received inviting him for an interview. Almost immediately, Pete received responses from all but one company saying that the positions had been filled. Pete looked at the company that said they were still willing to give him an interview and saw that the position was for a door-to-door fundraising position.

Frustrated at himself for having wasted so much time painting something that did little more than simply prove that Pete was not cut out to be an artist, he begrudgingly responded that he would attend the interview.

It was only a few minutes before he got an email back to confirm the interview time. The email also explained that as part of the interview process, he would go door-to-door with an experienced team of salesmen to ask for charitable donations. Pete closed his laptop and walked over to the painting of the boat in a storm that he had done.

For a brief moment Pete contemplated continuing to paint, but then looked out the window and noticed that the large, steel trash can on the street was, for the first time, completely empty and not overflowing with trash.

This is a sign, Pete reasoned.

Driven by anger and disappointment, Pete dragged his painting down the flight of stairs onto the street and threw it inside the trash can. The painting didn't really fit, but that wasn't his concern anymore.

Once back inside, Pete laid down in bed and stared at the white ceiling above him. His racing thoughts kept him from falling asleep. Pete knew that his inability to control his emotions was one of his greatest weaknesses.

What if I just made the wrong choice? Pete pondered. Exhausted by his overthinking, Pete eventually fell asleep and didn't wake up until the sun had come up the following morning.

Upon waking, Pete wondered if it had all been a dream. Then, he wondered if the painting was still where he had left it, awkwardly placed inside the steel trash can on the street just outside his window.

Pete leaped out of bed and almost slammed his face against the glass window in his hurry to look outside. The painting was gone.

***

It was one of the coldest nights of the year, and Pete was not dressed for the weather. The email had warned about the cold, but Pete thought he would be alright with just a cotton sweater and a blue corduroy blazer. Even if he had wanted to dress in a way that ensured he wouldn't feel the cold, Pete was used to dressing formally for interviews and felt it would have been strange to show up dressed as if he were going skiing.

However, the interview part of the recruitment process took only about ten minutes. Afterward, Pete was quickly assigned a fundraising team to follow, shadow, and learn from during his interview day.

Pete hated every moment of shadowing the team. He disliked how the people on the team spoke to each other as if they all belonged to a cult and then suddenly acted all cheerful and disingenuous the second they stood before a homeowner and asked for a charitable donation.

It was late, and Pete had been to more houses than he ever believed possible in a single day. He had met people of all ages and temperaments. Most people did not seem as frustrated with the fundraisers knocking at their door as Pete felt having to be one of them.

After stopping for a short break to eat something, Pete sat down with the rest of the fundraisers and drank his coffee as slowly as possible to try to thaw himself out.

Damien, the team leader, noticed how cold Pete was getting.

"Do you want to make a quick visit to the store so we can get you some gloves and a scarf, Pete?"Damien asked, looking slightly annoyed.

Pete had already decided that he would quit after getting dinner and before embarking on the next run of houses. As much as he wanted to find a suitable business job, and as confident as he was that he could ace the interview and become a full-time door-to-door fundraiser if he wanted, he felt that he would not get anywhere doing this type of work. However, he had also realized that he had no idea where he was and that he was indeed very cold. Rather than try to find whatever store Damien was referring to by himself, he decided to let Damien show him and then he'd leave the interview right after.

"Sure, thanks a lot," Pete replied as he took another generous swig of black coffee. He didn't usually drink coffee late in the evening, but he already knew that his mind was going to be racing this evening and, therefore, he would not be getting the quality sleep he needed.

Once everyone on the team finished their food and drinks, they all got up and were told by

Damien that they would be making a quick pit stop at the nearest shopping center so that Pete could get a scarf and some gloves. Pete made sure to look away to avoid any potential glares from the rest of the team, who surely wanted to go home as much as Pete did but still had a few more houses to visit.

Feeling slightly guilty and very cold, Pete and the rest of the team followed Damien to one of the largest shopping centers Pete had ever seen.

Not wanting to delay the group too much, Pete grabbed the nearest pair of gloves and scarf he could find and informed Damien that he was ready to pay. The entire team followed Pete and Damien to the cashier, where they encountered a seemingly endless line of people.

"Wow, that's a big line..." Pete said nervously, feeling very awkward and hating that he hadn't dressed appropriately for the weather. Damien didn't respond; he simply sighed and looked at his watch.

"I just hope the team gets to visit the five houses that need to be checked off the list before returning to the office," Damien said in a frustrated tone.

"I hope so too! Surely the queue will move quickly," Pete responded. The more he tried to think of a way to inform Damien that he would be quitting and not visiting any more houses, the more he realized there was no way of doing so without potentially making the other team members hate him even more than they probably already did.

After about twenty-five minutes, Pete finally arrived at the cashier and paid for his scarf and gloves.

"Well, now that Pete is appropriately dressed, we can continue. The unfortunate news is that we will not have time to visit all the houses we were supposed to. Looking at the time, it seems we only have enough time left to visit one," Damien explained. He purposefully avoided eye contact with Pete, who was hoping a hole would open up in the cement under his feet and swallow him whole. Everyone on the team was muttering things between each other that Pete wholeheartedly believed they were about him.

"Actually, Damien… I…" Pete began thinking of a way to quit that would allow him to avoid being lynched by the fundraisers.

"Yes, Pete?" Damien asked.

"Never mind… sorry for the delay," Pete said, ultimately deciding to preserve his integrity and follow the team to just one more house before going home and sending an email to the company thanking them for their consideration but informing them that he would not be continuing in the hiring process.

Damien ushered the team toward the last house of the day.

***

Damien knocked loudly on the door once and then retreated a couple of steps back. The house was very small and surrounded by luscious shrubbery; it seemed more like a cottage than a house. Pete half expected a wizard to answer Damien's knock. Instead, a large man in his late thirties opened the door. This man was wearing a holey T-shirt emblazoned with a band's logo along with a patchy beard that was in desperate need of grooming.

Before the man could ask who the group was, Damien once again explained that they were a team of fundraisers asking homeowners in the neighborhood for charitable donations. Pete kept thinking about how in a few seconds, this man would tell Damien to leave and Pete would no longer be subjected to Damien's fake fundraising voice.

"Alright, come in. It's cold. My name is Michael," the large man said as he stepped back and ushered the team inside his home.

Pete smiled, but inside, he was furious as he was desperate to go home.

Once inside, Pete noticed the soothing and welcoming scent of some sort of beef stew being cooked. The place was very cluttered, with books, bags, and small sculptures scattered all over the floor. That made the house seem even smaller than it already was.

"I live here with my wife, but she's not home yet. She's in an art expo, but she'll be home soon," Michael explained with a smile, seemingly happy to have visitors at his place.

As Damien explained the purpose of the charitable donation, Pete looked aimlessly around the house, as he had already done several times that day.

Almost immediately, he noticed something on the floor that caught his eye. His heart skipped a beat. Pete rushed forward and picked up the painting of the boat crossing a storm he had thrown away just a few days ago.

"Where did you get this?" Pete asked. Damien shot a look of disapproval at Pete, as he was not allowed to speak during these visits.

"My wife found it on the street one day while visiting a friend. She said it was beautiful and that she couldn't believe someone would just throw it away," Michael responded. "I don't know anything about art, but she's an expert, so I believe her. It's strange because no one signed it, though…"

Pete looked at the painting as if its colors were moving and speaking to him. Although the entire fundraising team was looking at Pete in utter confusion and disbelief, Michael once again seemed amused.

"It's funny because the last time I brought something home off the street, my wife got mad at me. It was a traffic sign just lying on the street that I thought would look funny in the living room. So, when she brought this home, I asked her why I wasn't allowed to bring things in off the street and she could. Of course, she explained that this wasn't just a street sign but a work of art..."

With every word Michael spoke, Pete's smile grew larger.

"You're wrong," Pete said. "It most definitely is a sign, and one that I will never ignore again."

Chapter 7

Five Stories About Adventure

The Flight

Eleanor had never been on a plane in her life. On the other hand, I had already lived in seven different countries before turning thirty. I had probably flown to visit my parents in Spain during my school breaks more times than Eleanor had driven across the country to visit her parents.

As we got ready and prepared to leave the apartment, I was excited to give Eleanor a positive first flying experience.

"I could get us to Spain with my eyes closed," I said, trying to assuage her nervousness.

"But I know I'm going to get nervous. You have to hold my hand when we take off!" Eleanor demanded.

"With pleasure!" I responded enthusiastically.

It had been years since I'd seen someone so nervous about flying, especially over a flight that was less than two hours long. Luckily, I knew what I was doing and found Eleanor's trepidation very sweet.

As we got on the express train that took us directly to the airport, I realized I had left my Spanish ID in the apartment.

"Does that mean we can't fly?" Eleanor asked nervously.

"No, it's ok. We can still make it. I'll take the train back home once we get to the airport," I replied. Luckily, I always arrived exceptionally early for flights. This time, I had planned to arrive three hours before takeoff just to make sure everything went smoothly and so I could show Eleanor around the airport that I had come to know so well.

Upon arriving at the station, we noticed black smoke emerging from the nose of the train. Shortly after, a woman came on the PA system and said that the train was on fire and everyone needed to deboard quickly, which we did.

"It's ok; I'll take a taxi!" I said hastily as Eleanor and I rushed into the airport and away from the black smoke.

Even though it was rush hour and it would take me two hours to get to the apartment and back, I got in the taxi. Eleanor stayed behind with the luggage in a café near where we had to check in, and I tried not to think about how much money the taxi ride was going to cost me.

I had been in the taxi for about thirty minutes when I realized that I had left the keys to the apartment in the luggage that was at the airport with Eleanor. When I informed the taxi driver, he took me back to the airport but still charged me the entire fee for the original trip.

When Eleanor saw me rushing toward her madly, she stood up in bewilderment.

"What happened?" she asked, clearly confused.

"The keys to the apartment are in the suitcase…" I replied despondently.

Eventually, we found a train that was not on fire and made it to the apartment, where I retrieved my Spanish ID. By the time we arrived back at the airport, we had already missed our flight and had to take a later one.

***

As the plane began to move, I reached toward Eleanor so that she could grab my hand tightly when her nerves kicked in. However, Eleanor turned to me with a relaxed smile and gently began caressing my hand.

"Aren't you nervous?" I asked.

"I would have been. But today was so hectic that now I have no energy left to be scared..." Eleanor replied before kissing me on the cheek and laughing.

DETOUR

It had been a long time since Marcus had gotten so drunk. The taxi driver had been giving him dirty looks ever since his friends poured him into the backseat and told the driver where to drop him off.

"I need to stop, please!" Marcus exclaimed. "I'm gonna throw up!"

The taxi driver did not hesitate to let Marcus out by the side of the road, where he sprinted toward the forest. At this time of night, the woods were completely dark and silent except for the sound of Marcus stumbling through the branches and twigs trying to find a place to vomit.

Once Marcus had rid himself of a small percentage of the alcohol currently coursing through his system, he could not find his way back to where the taxi had dropped him off. Regardless of where he turned, he just seemed to be going deeper and deeper into the woods—and since he'd only ever seen them from the road while driving past in the car, he didn't have a good sense of which way to go.

Eventually, Marcus returned to the road, but the taxi was no longer there. Instead, a garbage truck passed by and, seeing Marcus's disheveled state, offered him a ride to the nearest train station.

"I've never been in a garbage truck before!" Marcus mused, slurring his words so much that the two men driving him to the station couldn't help but laugh.

Once they dropped him off, Marcus ran to catch the train but missed it by a few seconds. He peered at the screen and finally managed to make out that this was the last train of the night. Determined to find the sanitation workers again and wanting to get as far away as possible from the strange men dressed in all-black hoodies at the other end of the station, Marcus ran back into the street and eventually ended up back in the woods.

Marcus stumbled through the woods again until he finally saw a chain-link fence that he recognized. It was the fence that separated the forest from the highway.

Marcus ran up the muddy hill and climbed the fence. Before jumping onto the highway, his jacket got stuck and ripped, leaving a massive hole on the left side of the coat.

A toll collector saw Marcus wandering next to the highway and allowed him inside the toll booth, then called a taxi to come pick Marcus up.

Once the taxi arrived, Marcus stumbled inside and fell asleep on the seat immediately.

"Do you know where you live, boy?" the man at the toll booth asked.

The taxi driver smiled and said, "I just had this guy in my cab, but he ran off into the woods! Don't worry. I'll get him home!"

Marcus woke up partway through the drive and tried to think of what he would tell his mother when she saw the state he was in.

"Just tell her a dog or something attacked you," the taxi driver suggested.

"And what about the smell of alcohol on me?" Marcus asked.

"Tell her the dog was Irish!"

BUSKING

Anna and I watched the busker perform fantastic music on his old, beat-up, acoustic guitar on the side of the street for what felt like an hour before he began talking to us and asking us about our lives.

"He plays guitar too!" Anna yelled, enthusiastically pointing at me—as if it wasn't clear who she was referring to.

"Is that so?" the busker asked as he handed me his guitar. He introduced himself as Morten and invited me to play.

Nervously, I accepted Morten's guitar and took his place on the little wooden seat he had been sitting on. Morten took a cigarette break and watched curiously to see what I could do on his instrument.

After about ten minutes of playing the songs I knew, Morten was impressed.

"I'm going to play at a bar in ten minutes. You guys should come with me!" he invited.

"Yes, we'd love to!" Anna replied. I was slightly nervous that he would ask me to play at this bar, but I agreed anyway. The three of us walked through the busy streets of Anna's hometown, which was filled with young people and older adults alike enjoying their Saturday night out on the town.

Once we arrived at the bar, Morten was greeted by many people who seemed bohemian and musical like him.

"You're on in five minutes!" Morten said as he handed me his guitar with a smile.

Anna once again leaped in excitement, but I was crippled with fear. The bar was not packed, but there was a table right next to the stage where a huge family was having a meal and some drinks.

Once I got on stage and connected the guitar to the amplifier, I told several jokes before getting started to loosen the tension I was feeling. Everyone looked at me as if they were worried that I would try to be a comedian all night instead of providing them with some live music.

After a deep breath, I began playing all the songs I knew, and in no time, everyone in the bar got up on their feet and started dancing and singing along.

It was one of the most exciting moments of my life, and although I probably played four or five songs, I felt like I had been playing for only a moment when Morten came up to me and asked for his guitar back.

I involuntarily hesitated to return the guitar to Morten, wanting to play longer, and he laughed.

"You got it now, huh?" he asked.

"Got what?" I queried.

"The performing bug!" he crowed.

I smiled and said, "Yeah, I guess I do. That was amazing!"

I sang and danced to every song Morten played, and when he was done, I asked if I could play a few more. He told me that he was going on tour in a week and asked if wanted to join him as he traveled through the country.

I looked at Anna, who, this time, did not jump up and down in excitement. That was the sign I needed to bring me back down to earth.

After that day, I began busking on the street every weekend. I eventually returned to the bar where I had played with Morten, and I'm there every Sunday night to this day.

BIRTHDAY

Andrea had fallen in love with Barcelona from the moment she and her dog, Bailey, landed in

Spain. After living in Germany her whole life, she immediately appreciated the warm climate and the feeling that if she lived in Barcelona, she would never need to go on vacation again.

Andrea had studied Spanish for most of her life, and this trip was aimed at completing the certification she needed to become an English teacher and to finally become fluent in Spanish. However, she found that she was too nervous to speak Spanish with the locals, so she constantly resorted to speaking English very slowly and using hand gestures.

When Andrea's friend Sophie wrote that she was going to visit Andrea for her birthday in a week, Andrea became ebullient. She would be able to speak German, or even English at a normal pace.

Andrea told her aunt Carina, who lived in Barcelona and was giving Andrea a place to stay, about Sophie's visit. "You must be so happy that your best friend is coming to visit you!" Carina exclaimed.

Andrea smiled. "Sophie is not my best friend, but maybe after this, she will be. It's lovely of her to come all the way here for a visit when she knows that I've been struggling with the language!"

A couple of days before Sophie was due to arrive, Andrea received a text saying that Sophie would be visiting Barcelona with her new boyfriend.

Andrea was unaware that Sophie even had a boyfriend and was unexcited about spending her birthday with a stranger, but she wrote back saying she was excited to meet him.

The night that Sophie landed, she, her boyfriend, and Andrea were meant to have dinner in a restaurant by the hotel where Sophie was staying.

Knowing that Bailey needed to be walked, Andrea decided to walk to the restaurant instead of taking the train even though it meant she would need to leave an hour earlier to arrive on time.

During their walk, Andrea surveyed everything around her as if taking mental photographs. The way people walked, talked, and did everything was different from what she was used to. The fact that she was minutes away from being reunited with someone who reminded her so much of home made her heart more open and receptive to everything this new city had to offer.

When Andrea was walking along the ocean, less than ten minutes away from arriving at the restaurant, she heard her phone beep to indicate a new text message had come in.

Sophie: Hi. Sorry, we are so tired after the flight. I think we are just going to go right to sleep. Can we meet up tomorrow instead? Thank you!

Andrea felt her heart sink. She wanted to throw the phone into the ocean on her left but instead replied that everything was OK. Except everything wasn't OK. Tomorrow was her birthday, and Andrea didn't want to feel this way on her last day of being 23.

Feeling too exhausted to walk back to her aunt's place, Andrea got on the metro despite her aunt's exhortation to never take the train late at night by herself. She had never used the metro before, but was convinced nothing could make her more upset than she already was.

Although she did not feel unsafe, she felt incredibly uncomfortable—like a sardine stuffed in a can. Many young and rowdy teenagers appeared to be using the metro as a jungle gym.

Bailey usually did not take kindly to loud strangers, but even he was too exhausted to protest. Andrea made herself as small as possible and glued her eyes to the map on the metro's wall that showed how many stops were left before she got off.

Andrea could hear her phone buzzing in her pocket with the specific ringtone she had designated for her parents. Unable to answer because doing so would mean elbowing someone, Andrea let it ring.

A large group of teenagers began aggressively shouting and taunting one another. Bailey started to growl, which prompted Andrea to put her hand on his muzzle. The last thing she needed was Bailey trying to participate in the hostilities.

It did not take long for the enraged youths to begin fighting each other in front of everyone. Even people who were just sitting quietly, like Andrea, got sucked into the chaos as they tried to get up from their seats to move away from the violence.

Andrea could not move because Bailey was now trying to free himself from her grip and it took all of her concentration to hang onto him. The metro doors opened. It still wasn't Andrea's stop, but she decided to get off anyway.

Just as she was almost entirely off the metro, Andrea felt someone accidentally shove her forward. Because she was cradling Bailey with both hands, Andrea couldn't grab on to anything or even brace for impact on the way down. She hit her head hard on the concrete floor.

If it hadn't been for Bailey barking manically, Andrea might have remained unconscious on the floor for much longer.

When she came to, she was flat on the floor and heard a male voice above her asking, "Can you stand up?"

Andrea looked up to see a boy roughly around her age, with kind brown eyes and messy black and gray hair.

Andrea slowly got up with the help of the kind stranger.

She did her best to answer his questions, but her mind was too fuzzy to comprehend what was happening.

"I'll take you to a hospital!" the boy said.

"No, I'm OK!" Andrea insisted.

"I think you might have a concussion!" he told her firmly.

"I'm fine, thank you." Andrea just wanted to go home and cry.

"At least take my number in case you need help with anything..." he persisted.

Andrea agreed to take the boy's number.

"What's your name?" she asked.

"José!"

***

The next morning, Andrea did end up going to the hospital with her aunt. It turned out that she did have a concussion, but she was allowed to go home later that evening.

Once she was out of the hospital, Andrea took Bailey to the vet to ensure nothing had happened to him in the altercation the night before.

"Andrea!" a somewhat familiar voice bellowed.

Andrea turned around to see the face of the boy who had helped her get off the floor after she fell in the metro station.

"José?" she said tentatively.

"You remember my name! Are you OK?" he asked.

José was wearing white scrubs and was holding a clipboard. He was a vet.

"Yeah, I'm OK. I'm here for Bailey!" Andrea responded, belatedly realizing it was clear that she would not go to a veterinary clinic to get herself checked.

José offered to take a look at Bailey himself.

In the meantime, Andrea was getting texts from Sophie asking Andrea if they could just celebrate her birthday in their hotel room since both Sophie and her boyfriend were still tired from the flight from Germany.

"My brother is opening a bar this evening in Alicante. It's a few hours away by car, and I'm driving alone. If you want, I could take you there for dinner, and then I'll drive you back home. Don't worry; I won't be drinking..." José offered.

Andrea smiled and replied that she would get back to him once she got home.

"OK, get home safe. Goodbye, Bailey!"

***

"But didn't you already buy a ticket to fly back to Germany in two days?" Carina asked Andrea after hearing about José's proposition.

Andrea was strongly considering the trip; after all, he was very handsome.

"Yeah, I know," Andrea said with a shrug.

"Does José know?" her aunt pestered.

"No," admitted Andrea.

"And what about Sophie? Would you rather go visit her, even despite how she is treating you?" continued Carina.

Everything Carina was asking was valid.

Andrea sat in her room and looked at her phone, as if waiting for someone to call her and let her know what to do.

José is very handsome, she thought.

Andrea smiled as she picked up her phone to type out a text.

> Andrea: José, I'd love to join you for the drive to Alicante tonight.

Sophie never texted again asking what happened or even to wish her a happy birthday, and anyway, Andrea was too excited and happy to feel bothered about her friend's indifference.

THE ROAD TRIP

"I don't understand. Why did you say no to seeing her again if you like her?" Natalie questioned her best friend José.

That is a good question, José thought.

"We had an amazing first date. We kissed and said we'd see each other again soon. When I woke up the next morning and saw the message from her telling me that she had been too scared to confess that she was leaving for Germany in two days, I knew this was my terrible luck ruining my life again!" José admitted.

"But if she was too scared to tell you, it's because she liked you! Especially if she said that she was willing to postpone her trip and stay here for you!" Natalie argued.

The more José tried to think of a counterargument, the more he realized how right his best friend was.

"Well, it's too late now anyways. She's back in Germany, and even if I wanted to fly there, I can't go because of Harley," José protested.

Harley was José's cocker spaniel. She was two years old and could not go on airplanes due to her short nose, which could cause breathing problems on the flight.

Natalia grinned at José as she put her coffee down on the circular wooden table between them and looked at him, satisfied.

"You have a car... and one you've been meaning to take on a road trip for some time now..." she coaxed.

Once again, she was right.

***

The drive from Spain to Germany was about eleven hours—and even longer with Harley in the backseat.

"So she has no idea you're coming. How do you even know where she lives?" asked Natalie.

"On our first date, we realized that she lived next door to a cousin of mine. My cousin already said he'd let me stay with him in case Andrea does not want to see me when I surprise her!" shared José.

Natalie helped José pack his things into the backseat of his blue SUV and settled Harley onto her favorite brown bed in the spacious cargo area.

"Ready?" Natalie asked as she looked at José through the passenger seat's open window.

José nodded and drove off to tell Andrea that he had changed his mind and understood why she had been nervous to tell him about her return flight to Germany.

As José and Harley left Spain and entered France, the sun was finally starting to rise over the horizon. It illuminated the intimidating trucks zooming past them and the verdant greenery in the surrounding fields.

José felt bad for Harley, who had no choice but to endure his terrible and impassioned singing for the entire journey. Luckily, Harley was very quiet for the first couple of hours, probably sleeping, which made him jealous.

José knew that driving tired was more dangerous than driving drunk, but he had started packing his bags late in the afternoon and only managed to get a few hours of sleep. He also wanted to arrive in Germany before Andrea went to sleep for the night.

Once the sun was completely out and the road no longer seemed like a new and exciting prospect, Harley and José began to feel exhaustion set in.

After enduring Harley's whining for about an hour, which was probably payback for having had to endure José's awful singing, the two of them stopped at a gas station in France.

He hadn't felt so foolish and powerless for a very long time as he did that morning trying to figure out how to put gas in his car in a foreign language. At one point, José may as well have been playing Tetris on the touch screen at the pump for all the good it was doing.

Finally, a kind, elderly man who was fueling up his car at the next pump came over to help, as he spoke English. He was surprisingly chatty, but José took advantage of the conversation as he thought about the hours of driving ahead of him.

"Why didn't you just call and tell the girl how you feel?" Idris, the elderly man, asked.

"I thought this would be more romantic," admitted José.

"That might be true, but I think you jumped a couple of steps ahead. Are you sure she feels the same way?" Idris asked.

Regardless of how much José tried to forget Idris's question, he found it hard to think about anything else for the rest of the drive.

The second stop happened once Harley began barking in the back. José parked the car in a gas station in Lyon and walked Harley through an expansive forest that was unfortunately filled with litter.

Harley was pulling on the leash so much that he decided to unleash her and let her run around the woods to burn off her extra energy. Almost immediately after unleashing his dog, José learned why Harley had been so interested in being set free.

"Leave the squirrel!" José screamed as he summoned the little energy he had acquired from the bitter yet expensive gas station espressos.

José ran through the woods, hoping that Harley wouldn't chase the squirrel in front of an oncoming truck. Eventually, he caught up with Harley, picked her up, and carried her back to the car, where he placed her in the trunk and informed her that because of her bad behavior, he would now sing the entire rest of the trip to Germany.

The rest of the trip was nowhere near as exciting as the first few hours, which made finally arriving at Andrea's place all the more thrilling. The entire trip, José had been worrying about what Andrea would think when seeing José. What if Idris was right? What if his recent behavior had made her lose interest in him and, therefore, she would not appreciate the romantic gesture he was about to complete?

José parked the car in front of Andrea's house and looked at his phone. He had several missed calls from Natalie, but he would have to reply to them some other time.

José got out of the car, leaving Harley and his luggage in the trunk. He couldn't remember feeling this nervous in a very long time. Continuing to ignore his phone buzzing inside his jeans pocket, José rang the doorbell and took a couple of tentative steps back.

A man in his late 40s answered the door and said something in German.

"Excuse me, is Andrea home?" José asked uncertainly.

The man continued to speak in German, so José took out his phone to translate when he received yet another call from Natalie.

"Nat, I can't speak right now. I need to translate something into German!" José exclaimed.

"Well, I have someone here who can probably help!" Natalie said as she turned her phone camera to show a very embarrassed-looking Andrea.

José's jaw dropped.

"Hi, José, is that my father behind you?" Andrea asked.

Judging by the man's ebullient smile when he saw Andrea on José's phone, it was clear that this man was obviously her father.

"So, I guess we were both thinking of the same way to surprise each other. Only, I stayed a few more days without telling you so that I could surprise you…" Andrea explained.

José looked at the picture on his phone in disbelief, then smiled.

"So, you're not angry at me?" he asked.

"Of course not. I wanted to show you that I liked you and that I was sorry I didn't tell you about my flight home, which I canceled for you!" exclaimed Andrea.

As Andrea's dad took the phone and began speaking to his daughter, Jose let out a deep sigh of relief. Now the only question was how to get back to Spain.

CHAPTER 8

FIVE STORIES ABOUT THE GOLDEN YEARS

PHOTO ALBUM

Nathan sat on his black leather couch, perusing the photo album his son had made for him for his 80th birthday a few days ago. The day had been very hectic with everyone running around the house and bringing Nathan presents before his big birthday dinner.

Things had quieted down now, and it was the time in the afternoon when Nathan usually sat on his old sofa that he'd had for over twenty years and rested his feet. Originally, the sofa had been placed in front of the big window where Nathan could look out over the large, carefully maintained front yard and the quiet street beyond.

A few years ago, though, Nathan decided to turn the couch around to face away from the window. He had started to feel self-conscious about falling asleep and having the neighborhood children see him with his eyes closed and mouth open.

As Nathan opened the impressively heavy photo album, he noticed the noise he detested hearing when sitting on his couch: the booming and obnoxious sound of children playing surprisingly close to his window.

Rather than turning around to see exactly what was going on, Nathan continued flipping the pages of his photo album. It did not take long for him to become fully immersed in the photographs. As he looked through them, the photos took him back to every memory they showed.

Nathan had one son—William. William was the father of three rowdy, lively young boys who had spent the entire birthday weekend running up and down Nathan's house as if it were the most exciting theme park they had ever seen. One of the main reasons why Nathan was so happy to be sitting on his sofa was that he hadn't managed to have a quiet moment to himself ever since William and the children had been home. However, the noise outside was starting to break Nathan's concentration.

Turning the album's pages, Nathan saw photos of himself when he was about thirty years younger—before William was even dating the woman who would later become his wife and the mother of his three energetic children.

The more Nathan perused the album, the quieter everything around him became and the more he smiled. Nathan stopped turning the pages and started to reminisce about the past.

Nathan remembered how there used to be a time when William was even more willful and defiant than his three boys. Nathan smiled when he realized that he, himself, had probably been the worst of all as a child.

As Nathan reached the last page of the album, he felt his heart ache. He wished that the album was longer or that there was another one for him to look through so that he could continue reminiscing about moments from the past that he'd forgotten about.

Nathan closed the album and gently ran his fingers across the beige leather as if the album was a living thing. As if still looking through the pictures, Nathan's mind began running through very vivid memories of his time with William as a child and with William's children when they were too young to walk, much less sprint and leap the way they currently did. His thoughts made the sounds outside his window disappear completely, until he heard someone call his name.

Nathan slowly got up from his sofa and walked over to the window. William and his three boys were outside in his yard, running around like they usually did.

"Hey, Dad! The boys wanted to see you again. They said they missed you! I just know they can be a lot, so we decided to play outside in your yard to burn off some energy before we come inside. I hope that's ok." William cried as his three children ran circles around his legs.

Nathan smiled broadly and waved at his son to let him know everything was fine.

All three boys waved at Nathan excitedly, as if it had been years since they'd seen him rather than a day.

Still smiling, Nathan returned to his sofa. But instead of sitting down, he turned it around to face the window. For the first time in many years, he could look out into the front yard of his house from his seat on the black leather sofa. Although he'd already looked through the whole photo album, now he could look out over the memories he was making that very moment by watching his son and his three rowdy grandchildren, who were genuinely excited to see him every day, playing outside his window.

THE BREAKFAST ORDER

Nathan and his oldest grandchild, Jake, who was six years old at the time, were sitting opposite each other at a diner just a couple blocks away from Nathan's apartment.

Jake loved visiting the US because it meant he and his family could stay at Nathan's apartment there. Nathan didn't live in the United States either, but he had a small apartment that he mainly visited during the summer. This year,

Nathan had invited his son William and the rest of William's family to join him at the apartment and spend a couple of weeks there during the summer holidays.

Jake had been woken up by his grandfather, who asked Jake if he wanted to go to breakfast at the diner nearby. Jake loved his grandfather a lot, and his grandfather often played together with Jake as if they were the same age, but the two of them rarely spent time alone together.

Finding no reason to say no, Jake got up and dressed as quickly as possible. The two of them walked over to the diner Jake always saw when visiting his grandfather's apartment, but had yet to eat in. Jake's father William had become overly fastidious about what Jake could eat and drink, and he primarily ate vegetables and drank water—maybe sometimes milk if he was lucky. Therefore, sitting in a classic American diner with his grandfather filled Jake with excitement as he pondered all the possible things he would be allowed to eat.

Jake laughed just looking at the menu, which was almost too big for him to even hold. The menu was laminated in plastic and covered in ketchup and other mysterious, food-looking stains, which made Jake all the more excited to eat there. The menu also had big pictures of some of the foods, which Jake focused on exclusively without even reading what the dishes actually were.

A red-haired waitress with large, round glasses and a nametag that read "Janet" came up to their table and spoke to them in a very enthusiastic tone. She greeted Nathan and Jake as if they were guests of honor and asked what they wanted to eat.

Nathan ordered first, and Janet repeated his choice as she scribbled on her notepad.

"Thank you. That sounds great," Nathan confirmed.

"And what can I get you, young man?" Janet inquired.

"I'll have the XL breakfast platter!" Jake exclaimed excitedly.

Janet and Nathan looked at each other with similar expressions of mild concern.

"That is a very big platter. Are you sure you can eat it? It has pancakes with—" Janet began.

"Yes, I'm sure!" Jake enthused.

"Jake, your dad says sometimes you order more than you can eat. Maybe we should ask Janet if there are other options more suited to you. Why don't you look at the menu and read everything you're ordering?" suggested Nathan.

Janet smiled and was about to recommend other dishes to Jake when she was interrupted again.

"No, that's what I want, and I don't want anything else!" Jake demanded.

Nathan looked at his grandchild, surprised at his mild outburst. Janet smiled again and made her way to the kitchen.

"You know, sometimes it's good to listen to people. Even if we think we are right, it does not always mean we are…" Nathan tried to explain to his grandchild, who shrugged and seemed disinterested.

"I'm gonna eat all of it!" insisted Jake.

"And what if you don't?" prompted Nathan.

Jake looked at all the delicious food around him and was convinced that he would have no problem putting away the XL breakfast platter.

"Then I'll go and clean the kitchen of the diner!" Jake finally suggested, to which Nathan chuckled quietly.

When the food finally arrived, Nathan and Jake marveled at how Janet masterfully balanced the enormous platter of pancakes, bacon, eggs, and toast.

"This is for you, young man," Janet said as she very slowly lowered the meal that seemed large enough to feed an entire family.

Jake eyed the enormous meal enthusiastically, especially the creamy sphere on top of his towering stack of pancakes.

"Ice cream!" Jake cried as he looked at the puffy scoop.

Nathan smiled. "Jake, can I give you some advice about what you're about to eat?"

Jake shot his grandfather a frustrated look and shook his head emphatically. Nathan kept silent, but couldn't help continuing to smile.

After contemplating the massive breakfast as if it were some trophy that had just been awarded to him, Jake grabbed a spoon and took a big scoop of the "ice cream" on top of his pancakes.

Almost immediately after putting the scoop in his mouth, Jake made a face like he had just tasted something much worse than the vegetables his father encouraged him to eat on a daily basis.

"Already figured out that it's pure butter and not ice cream?" Nathan asked, trying very hard not to laugh.

Jake spat out the butter onto his plate and took a big gulp of his drink.

***

"Thank you for not making me clean the kitchen," Jake said as he and his grandfather walked home from the diner.

Nathan was carrying pretty much everything Jake had been served for breakfast in a plastic takeout container.

"It's OK. As long as you learned an important lesson then it's completely fine," Nathan reassured him.

"I did. Next time, spread the butter on something first!" Jake exclaimed as he put his arm around his grandfather and headed home.

DISCIPLINE

Grandpa Albert was waiting in line with his son and grandson Nathan at the Italian restaurant in the airport. Nathan and Albert had a very special connection where they were constantly playing pranks on people and telling silly jokes that no one else found as funny as they did.

Much to Nathan's dismay, his winter break was over and it was time to go home, which meant he had to say goodbye to his grandfather. Grandpa Albert had accompanied them to the airport to wish Nathan and the rest of the family goodbye.

During the entire car ride to the airport, Nathan and Grandpa Albert were reminiscing about all the fun stuff they did together and all the fun things they wanted to do next time Nathan and his family were in town.

Once the entire family had ordered their food, they all took their trays and sat together at a table close to the TV screen that would announce when their flight would begin boarding.

"Nate," Nathan's dad Mike said as he nudged his oldest son, "can you give a slice of pizza to your little brother?"

Nathan's little brother, Zach, who was only a couple of years younger than he was, reached out to grab a slice from Nathan, who immediately pulled his pizza away in anger.

"No!" Nathan declared.

Grandpa Albert smiled. "C'mon, Nate. He's hungry and you know that you got the last pizza they had…"

Zach slammed his small fists against the wooden table in frustration.

"He can't have any of my pizza!" Nathan exclaimed angrily as he took another bite of his margherita pizza.

Even Grandpa Albert looked unimpressed this time.

Normally, Grandpa Albert always sided with Nathan and ensured he got what he wanted at all times due to the strong bond they had. However, this time, he was visibly frustrated at Nate's reluctance to share his pizza with his younger brother.

Grandpa Albert almost said something to his grandson, but then realized he didn't want to create trouble. Albert lived a pretty solitary life, and he always got a lot of grief from his children about how he had to be more conscious of his health and many other things. However, with his grandson Nate, there was nothing to worry about other than having fun—and that made him reluctant to ruin their relationship by trying to discipline Nathan in any way.

Nate ate the pizza so enthusiastically that it seemed as if he was eating just to keep the food away from his little brother rather than to satiate his own hunger.

Grandpa Albert became so troubled by Nathan's behavior that he had to stand up and go for a quick walk. Albert had never felt like his grandson had done anything wrong before, and would often come to his defense whenever Nate's parents were angry at him about something. This made his disappointment all the more frustrating.

"Grandpa!" Nathan called out as he ran up behind Albert.

"Yes?" answered Albert.

"I need your advice!" Nate explained.

"What is it?" asked Albert.

"I wanted to give my little brother a slice of pizza, but I didn't like the way he just tried to take it without me even answering him. I wanted

Dad to tell Zach not to be rude but instead he got angry at me! I don't want Zach to be hungry, but I didn't like how Dad got angry at me and not at Zach for trying to take my pizza before I could even say if he could have some. What should I do?"

Grandpa Albert smiled as he felt a heavy weight fall off his shoulders. Suddenly, everything became clear to him. His role was not to discipline; instead, it was one that he felt a lot more excited about—to advise.

Looking at his grandson, Albert knew that Nathan would never have confided this information to his father and that he ran to ask his grandfather for advice because of the trust they shared.

Albert put his hand on his grandson's shoulder. The two of them walked through the airport and conversed about the situation. Grandpa Albert never disciplined Nate but merely advised him, which was endlessly more gratifying to him.

HUMBERTO

Nathan had always preferred his Grandpa Albert to his Grandpa Humberto. Albert was his father's father, and Nathan loved playing games with him so much that Nathan even preferred spending time with his grandpa rather than with his own friends from school.

Humberto was his mother's father. Humberto was slightly older and was a much more stoic and stern man. Nathan had never seen him angry, but had also never seen him express any emotion.

Nathan sat down to watch his favorite film with the entire family one day, which happened to be a particularly emotional film that always made everyone cry, and noticed that Humberto hadn't shed a single tear. After that moment, Nathan considered his grandfather Humberto utterly devoid of emotion, which was the complete opposite from Grandpa Albert.

One day, Humberto's small cocker spaniel got really sick and had to be taken immediately to the vet, where the doctor said that the dog was very ill and also too old to survive the surgery he needed to get.

Nathan and his parents were at the vet with Humberto when the doctor presented this horrible news. Nathan looked at Grandpa Humberto and was shocked to see that he didn't shed a single tear over the fate of his lifelong companion.

"I can't believe Grandpa didn't even cry about his dog's diagnosis," Nathan said once he got home and was alone with his parents.

"Nathan, your grandfather cannot cry. He has dry eye syndrome," Nathan's mother explained.

"What?" Nathan cried, never having heard of such a thing.

"It's true," Nathan's dad added, "but he cries inside every time you leave his house after visiting."

Nathan pondered the news he had just been given.

**

The next day, Nathan walked all the way to visit Grandpa Humberto by himself. Once he was inside, Nathan sat with him all day and listened to his grandpa talk about his cocker spaniel and how he was afraid the dog would have to be put down.

Although Grandpa Humberto did not shed a tear, this time Nathan knew what he was feeling inside.

BOXED FEELINGS

George had been living with his grandfather, Harold, for several years. The house they lived in was small, but since George's parents could no longer look after him, this was the best alternative.

The house was situated in a semirural part of town filled with trees, neatly maintained lawns, and people mostly over the age of 60. George spent most of his free time trying to find work to afford his own place, but he was in his last year of high school, which meant that he had to divide his time between studying for his exams and trying to find a suitable university to attend.

Lately, George had been finding it challenging not to feel overwhelmed by everything—something Harold had noticed immediately. Harold came from a generation of people who did not speak about their feelings, and George found it hard to contain his emotions.

Wanting to help his grandson feel better, Harold approached George one day after George got home from school with an idea for how to handle his frustrations.

George entered the house with a solemn expression on his face.

"George, I have an idea," Harold declared. He was wearing his usual flannel shirt and oversized jeans as he looked excitedly at George.

"Hi, Grandad; what is it?" George asked.

Harold extended his left hand to point out a cardboard box resting on a small wooden table by the front door to George.

"What is that?" George questioned.

"That is the box where you are to drop off all your frustrations when you walk through this door," Harold explained as he pointed to the yellow legal pad resting by the box. "You grab a piece of paper, and you write down your frustrations and put them in the box. That way, you leave all your worries behind when you come into this house. You are not to open the box at any point because that would mean you are allowing your frustrations back into your heart. Once the box gets filled up, we empty everything inside and start from scratch!"

Harold was very proud of his idea. He had been struggling to devise ways to help rid his grandson of his worries to no avail. The more he hoped George would discover how to feel better on his own, the worse George seemed to become. Harold knew George needed help, but he hadn't been exactly sure what to do.

"You really think that's going to help me?" George asked, somewhat bemused.

"I really do! It's something my parents used to do with me. No one is ever allowed to open it; we only empty it once it is full," said Harold.

Looking nonplussed, George agreed to use the box. He immediately wrote something down on a sheet of yellow paper, folded it, opened the cardboard lid, and placed the paper inside the box.

"Perfect!" Harold exclaimed, convinced that this would help put a smile on his grandson's face again. "Now, just leave your troubles inside that box and focus on the things that you need to do. I'll give you your space."

For the next few days, George's mood did not seem to improve. Harold was disappointed his idea hadn't worked and unsure about what to do next. He sat in his room and wondered what to do to help his grandson, but no matter how hard he tried to think of something, he failed to come up with a new idea that he felt would work.

After a couple of weeks of watching George become increasingly frustrated with his workload, Harold decided to open the box and see what George had written and put inside— even though that was something that was against the rules of the box.

The note read:

I am frustrated because I wish my grandad would ask me about my worries and talk to me, other than require that I ignore them completely. And if you are reading this, then you are breaking your own rules, grandad.

Less than five minutes after Harold opened the box, George walked through the front door and saw his granddad reading his note.

"You're cheating…" George said with a mocking half-smile.

"And you're right about what you wrote. I'm sorry," Harold apologized.

That evening, Harold and George sat down to talk for the first time in many years. George confessed that he felt lonely and isolated living in Harold's house, and Harold admitted that he recognized that he should have been more communicative with George.

After Harold and George came to an understanding, the box was put in the recycling bin, but the legal pad and pen were left where they were by the door.

"It seems that writing down our thoughts wasn't such a bad thing; maybe we just need to leave them out in the open instead of putting them in a box," suggested George.

Harold smiled and agreed.

***

The next day, Harold came downstairs to have breakfast and saw something written on the legal pad by the door. He bent over to read it:

Went to buy eggs. Writing notes that aren't part of a secret plan is not as fun as the ones that are, but I still like this idea. Maybe I'll become a writer or a negotiator after this. Thank you for caring about me. Love, George.

Chapter 9

Five Funny and Uplifting Stories

The Frog Boy

Stevie was sitting in the hotel lobby next to his parents with a giant smile on his face. It was the third and final day of the family's visit to his favorite theme park. He had already gone on all his favorite rides at least twice and eaten more hot dogs and pizzas than he had ever consumed at any other point in his life.

His parents had also enjoyed the experience, but it was time to drive back home. As Stevie sat on the red sofa decorated with imaginary, fantastical characters from the movies he loved watching, he reflected on all the fun he'd had at the park.

"What was your favorite part?" Stevie's mother asked him.

"I loved the show! The one where the prince saves the princess from the dragon and the castle!" enthused Stevie.

At night, once most of the rides had closed, there was a spectacle in the middle of the theme park where actors dressed as knights, princes, and monsters put on an open-air show filled with music and lights that made it feel as if everyone was inside a fantasy movie.

The more Stevie talked about it, the more excited he got about coming back next year.

Stevie didn't share with his mother how infatuated he had become with the actress who played the princess. When he watched the show over the past two nights, Stevie's heart had fluttered when she appeared in the castle window and pleaded for a prince to come and save her, which inevitably happened at the end of each show.

Before Stevie could say more about how much he loved the theme park, he saw a young girl about his age walk into the hotel reception area with her parents and a slightly older boy dressed all in black with gel in his hair—something Stevie thought only adults could wear.

The girl was blonde and looked a little like the princess from the evening shows. Stevie and the girl exchanged a glance before Stevie's father mentioned one of the very few things that could have distracted Stevie from the girl he had already deemed "the young princess" in his head.

"Stevie, would you like to go to the souvenir shop?"

As it happened, Stevie had been eyeing a plastic sword since the day they'd arrived at the hotel and passed the gift shop.

Sprinting past his father, who followed at a more sedate pace, Stevie raced to the store and found only one sword left.

"The last one..." Stevie said ominously to himself as he admired the sword and ran his finger carefully across the plastic blade as if it could cut him.

Stifling a laugh, Stevie's father took the sword and walked over to the cashier.

Waiting patiently by his father's side, Stevie noticed that he could still see the young princess in the lobby. When the older boy in black noticed them looking at each other, he stuck his tongue out at Stevie defiantly. Once again, the girl and Stevie exchanged glances.

Stevie shot a concerned look at his father to see if he had noticed this surprising interaction, but he hadn't.

Once the entire family was reunited on the sofa, Stevie began brandishing his sword bravely at the boy in black, who he had now mentally deemed "the dragon."

As Stevie's parents talked quietly, Stevie's imagination ran wild. He recalled all the amazing scenes from the nightly show and how appreciative the princess had been when the prince rescued her.

Stevie looked at his new sword and realized that it was up to him to recreate the fantastic story acted out the past three nights in the show.

Stevie swallowed his fear and gripped the sword tightly and courageously before making his way to stand before the dragon boy and challenge him for the right to save the princess.

As if the little girl and the boy in black knew precisely what was occurring, the princess looked worriedly at the boy in black, who began squaring up to Stevie.

He doesn't have a weapon; he has no chance against me, Stevie thought. However, the dragon boy did not seem bothered by the fact that Stevie was slashing the air in front of him with his sword as he approached.

The dragon boy quickly stepped in front of Stevie and began speaking loudly in a foreign language. Although Stevie could not understand what the dragon boy was saying, his tone communicated that it was hostile.

As Stevie brandished his sword, the dragon boy took out a toy laser that he had probably purchased at the park.

Intimidated by the weapon, Stevie looked at the princess and noticed she was looking on worriedly. Stevie knew this was his chance to impress her and prove that he was not scared of the laser he had contemplated asking his father to buy him before opting for the sword instead.

The dragon boy smiled and pointed the toy laser at Stevie. The toy weapon made sounds and lit up with different colors, making it clear that lasers were being fired.

Stevie jumped up in the air as far as he could each time the dragon boy shot a laser beam at him, making it clear that he was dodging each laser with his athletic prowess—something the young princess would surely admire.

Upon seeing Stevie's strategy for evading the imaginary laser shots, the dragon boy began laughing as loud as he could while pointing at him.

"Frog boy!" the boy exclaimed in a strange accent.

Stevie felt embarrassed. Before he could say anything back, the dragon boy walked off with the little blonde girl and left Stevie standing by himself with his sword.

"What was that about?" Stevie's mother asked him as he sat back down on the red sofa with his parents.

"I don't want to talk about it," Stevie replied.

A few moments later, Stevie got up and followed his parents to the restaurant they had been waiting to get into so they could have dinner as a family after a long day of enjoying rides at the park.

Throughout dinner, Stevie kept eyeing his sword, questioning if it were as powerful as he believed it would be.

"You don't like it?" Stevie's father asked as he lifted a slice of pepperoni pizza to his mouth.

"I do. I just don't know if I should have it. It's supposed to be used by a prince, and I couldn't even defeat a dragon," mumbled Stevie.

Whether they understood what he was talking about and knew things were not as grave as Stevie believed or were simply too confused to ask, Stevie's parents resumed their dinner after assuring him that if he wanted to be a prince, then he was a prince.

Although he appreciated the sentiment, Stevie felt disappointed after being mocked by the dragon boy and failing to be the prince he thought the little blonde girl needed.

Once dinner was over, Stevie and his parents exited the Italian restaurant and headed to the elevator to go up to their room and grab their luggage.

"Stevie, where is your sword?" his mother asked.

"I left it in the restaurant. I don't deserve it," replied Stevie.

"Of course you do. Go and get it before someone takes it!" his mother admonished.

Feeling disheartened, Stevie reluctantly returned to the restaurant and walked over to the booth he had been sitting in with his family, where he had forced down some spaghetti— Stevie always struggled to eat when he was upset.

Upon returning to the booth, he found his sword still on the floor. Strangely, he had been hoping someone had taken it.

Stevie lifted the sword and turned around to leave the restaurant.

In front of him stood the little blonde girl he'd seen earlier, but without the boy with the laser toy this time.

"I thought you were amazing," she said before kissing him on the cheek.

Before Stevie could say anything, the little girl smiled, turned around, and left.

Stevie stood in shock for a moment, then ran as fast as he could to meet his parents.

When they asked him what had excited him, Stevie held up the sword proudly before them as if the confrontation from earlier had never happened.

"The dragon boy was right. I was a frog before, but now I am a prince because the princess kissed me!" he exclaimed.

As if this declaration was all the explanation his parents needed, Stevie jumped in the air with his sword. He knew he would never leave it behind again now that he had been transformed from a frog to a prince because of the kiss he could still feel on his cheek.

LATE-NIGHT MOVIE

Joseph Sr. was coming home from a long day at the office. Although it had been a particularly trying day, filled with laboriously long meetings that seemingly culminated in nothing productive, he smiled.

As Joseph Sr. stopped the car at a red light, he looked down at the empty passenger seat and gleefully contemplated the reason for his good mood. On the seat next to him was a DVD box set with all of the films starring his eight-year-old son's favorite comedic actor. During his lunch break, Joseph Sr. had walked past an entertainment store and saw the box set. He immediately realized that this would be something his son would very much appreciate having, so he walked in and purchased it, excited to see what kind of reception he would have at home once he arrived with one of the best gifts he could imagine giving his son Joseph Jr.

Joseph Sr. had been working a lot lately and felt very disconnected from his family, especially his son. Every night he arrived home late from work, Joseph Jr. was already in bed. In the morning, Joseph didn't get to spend time with his son because, according to his wife, Joseph Jr. was having trouble sleeping at night.

That meant he struggled to get up on time for school and usually lay in bed for longer than he was supposed to.

Joseph wanted to find a way to help his son get the rest he needed, but he was too busy with work to focus on his son's issue. What worried him most was wondering if his son was struggling to sleep because of Joseph Sr.'s absence most of the week, even on weekends, due to his heavy workload.

Once Joseph got home, he entered the house and immediately presented his son with the box set. Joseph Jr. bounced around the house and screamed excitedly at the top of his lungs.

"Can we watch it now?! Please?!" Joseph Jr. begged his parents, holding onto the box so tightly it looked like he was scared a gust of wind would blow it away.

Joseph Sr. looked at his wife to see her look of disapproval.

"I would love to, but you need to get some sleep. You have school tomorrow, and it's not good to show up tired," Joseph declared, wondering if perhaps it had not been a wise choice to bring home the box set on a school night.

After a few more attempts to convince his parents to let him watch the DVDs, Joseph seemed to finally acquiesce to their wishes and disappeared to his room.

Less than ten minutes after running upstairs to his room without the box set, Joseph Jr. sprinted back down the stairs into the kitchen with unprecedented resolve. Seeing his son so keyed up made Joseph Sr. understand why it was hard for his son to sleep at night. In fact, it did not take long for Joseph Sr. to seriously contemplate the notion that the set of DVDs had only served to exacerbate the issue severely.

Joseph Sr. sat down at his desk and began to look through his emails before going to bed.

"I brought you a whiskey!" Joseph Jr. exclaimed as he suddenly emerged from behind his father, holding up a glass much too big for whiskey and filled to the brim as if it were apple juice.

"What is this for?" wondered Joseph Sr.

"I thought you might want some whiskey!" Joseph Jr. exclaimed. Joseph bewilderedly looked at his son, unsure of how he even knew where the whiskey was kept. It had been months since he had had a drink after work, but he felt oddly guilty refusing to take the glass from his son considering how he had wanted to reconnect with Joseph Jr. for so long.

"Thank you…" Joseph Sr. replied as he carefully took the overfilled glass and gingerly lowered it onto the desk.

As the night progressed, Joseph Jr. continued to perform small gestures seemingly aimed at making his father's evening more comfortable.

"Hi, dad; I brought you some slippers so you can keep your socks clean!" Joseph exclaimed as he proudly dangled some fluffy, pink slippers before his father. "Those belong to your mother!" Joseph Sr. responded, trying to stifle a laugh. Ultimately, he decided to wear them to humor his son, who was clearly trying to bribe his way into being able to watch the DVDs that evening.

As Joseph Sr. turned off his laptop and headed downstairs to eat something, wearing his pink, fluffy slippers and carrying a now-empty glass of whiskey, he arrived at the kitchen table to see a tall glass of beer and a cheese sandwich waiting for him.

Joseph Sr. had intended to heat up the dinner his wife had left him in the fridge, so he was surprised to see two slices of bread with an excessive amount of cheese in between resting on his wife's fine china, which she only used when they entertained very high-profile guests.

"Is that your mother's fine china?" asked Joseph Sr.

"Yes, and that is the finest sliced bread with cheese, just for you!" replied Joseph Jr. proudly.

Joseph Sr. eyed the tall glass of beer and worried that if the evening continued this way, a cheese sandwich would not be enough to soak up all the alcohol his son was presenting him with.

This time, he left the drink untouched, but he did eat the sandwich, which was the first thing he had ever seen Joseph Jr. make. Joseph Sr. winced when he realized there was a thick layer of ketchup over each slice of cheese.

After cleaning up his plate and putting the beer in the fridge, Joseph Sr. began to head upstairs to the bedroom when his son jumped in front of him, blocking the way.

"I put your pajamas in the washer so you can sleep with fresh clothes!" he enthused.

"In the washer?" Joseph Sr. inquired.

"Yes, mom showed me how. They should be ready in three hours," crowed Joseph Jr.

Joseph Sr. could not help but smile.

"I was kind of hoping to go to bed now, son…" he said gently.

"It's OK. I'll ask mom if you can borrow hers, so stay right here!" his son enthused.

"Son!" Joseph Sr. exclaimed.

"Yes?" he said.

"Let's watch one of those DVDs," Joseph Sr. said with a smile.

If his son was willing to go through all of this hard work, he at least deserved to watch one comedy.

Joseph Jr. bellowed with joy and quickly ran to the TV room to get ready.

***

Joseph Sr. put on the DVD and sat on the sofa with his arm around his son. He knew he would probably get reprimanded by his wife for turning on the movie, so he hoped after one film, Joseph Jr. would be too tired to ask to watch another.

Still wearing his fluffy pink slippers and feeling slightly light-headed from the whiskey, Joseph Sr. watched the first 10 minutes of the film before looking at his son, wondering why he wasn't laughing yet.

Joseph Jr. was fast asleep. His head was nestled on his father's chest, and his mouth was wide open. Although this was not what he thought would happen, Joseph Sr. smiled and continued watching the film. He kissed his son on the top of his head and rejoiced that his son was finally getting the sleep he needed after tiring himself out trying to bribe his father into watching the film.

Once the film finished, Joseph Sr. carried his son, who remained sound asleep, up to bed. Joseph Sr. arrived at his bedroom worried about what his wife might say but noticed that she was smiling just as much as he was.

"You're not mad?" he asked tentatively.

"No," his wife replied, "but you might be after you see what your pajamas look like now…"

"What happened?" he asked.

"Your son washed something red with your white pajamas, so now everything is bright pink," she explained.

Joseph Sr. laughed. "Well, at least now they match my fluffy slippers."

GDSF

Jake had never been to the youth club where everyone from his school hung out on the weekends. He'd always heard people talking about the club and the fun stuff they did there over the weekend, though.

Jake was very introverted and generally didn't like social settings, but one day after school, a couple of his friends said they would play cards at the social club on Saturday.

"Aren't there, like, teachers there and stuff?" Jake asked as he waited for his mom to pick him up at the school entrance.

"Yeah, but they don't care about anything. I think the teachers just go to get away from their significant others. They don't have to teach us anything, and there are some parents there too, so it's not like they are responsible for us either," Zachary responded, one hand gripping the padded strap of his red backpack.

"I heard that Ms. Thomas showed up drunk and told Doug about all the guys she's dated. It gets pretty wild there," Dean added excitedly.

"Are you serious?" Zachary asked incredulously.

"Yeah. She just sat there and listed all the men I hate for being lucky enough to date her."

"So that's your idea of a fun Saturday night? Sitting around with your geography teacher, hearing about her love life?" Jake inquired.

"Yeah! You got anything better to do?" Zachary responded.

The truth was, Jake had no plans other than staying home and sleeping. Jake was unconvinced that things would be as enjoyable as his friends made them out to be, but he had no plans, and if there were teachers around, then it couldn't be that intimidating.

***

The youth center was busier than any of the bars Jake and his friends had snuck into occasionally during weekends. There was music playing, but you couldn't hear the words of the song because everyone was talking so loudly at the same time.

There were people of all ages engaged in different activities. There was a round table filled with students playing cards with teachers, three large red sofas creating a semicircle around a large TV screen showing age-appropriate films, and a bar where you could order any soft drink you wanted (but no alcohol).

"I told you this would be awesome, didn't I?" Zachary asked with a satisfied grin on his face as he wiped his round glasses on his white, button-down shirt.

"It looks like every Thanksgiving I've ever had rolled into one place," Jake replied, unsure of how he felt about it.

Jake looked around and saw some people from his high school laughing and genuinely seeming to have a good time. It didn't take long before people started coming up to him and engaging him in conversation. After about an hour, Jake realized that, shockingly, he was having a good time.

For most of the evening, Jake sat on the sofa and watched movies, since he was an avid cinephile. Zachary and Dean were following Ms. Thomas around and asking her about her life before becoming a teacher, which was obviously making her somewhat uncomfortable.

After a couple of hours, Jake was ready to find his friends and say goodbye before heading home. Before he could begin searching for them, though, they found him.

"Jakey! We're playing GDSF! Come join us!" Zachary exclaimed.

"You're playing what?" asked Jake.

"Garbage Dump Skateboard Football, of course!" retorted Zachary.

Jake was now even more confused than before.

Rather than explain, Zachary and Dean dragged Jake outside to the building's driveway. There was a pretty steep slope, and at the bottom were two garbage dumpsters a couple of feet from each other.

"The idea is to release the skateboard and try to make it go between the dumpsters. If it goes through, then you get the point!" Dean exclaimed as Jake watched kids from his school release the skateboard and get frustrated when it smashed against one of the garbage dumpsters.

It took about ten minutes before it was finally Jake's turn.

As Jake was handed the skateboard, he noticed four of the most popular kids from his school walk up.

"What are they doing here?" Dean asked, frustrated.

"I heard they have to come at least once a month as a requirement for being on the basketball team. What are the chances they would come today!" muttered Zachary.

"OK, I'm pretty sure we shouldn't be playing this game, and I'm not gonna do this in front of the popular kids!" Jake said and started to hand the skateboard to someone else. Before he could escape from the game, Bash, one of the new arrivals and arguably the most popular guy in his school, approached. He asked Jake why he was bailing from the game, to which Jake had no response.

"Then let's do it, because I ain't going back inside to play cards with the teachers or to order an orange juice from the bar," Bash said as he stood directly in front of Jake.

Jake turned around and began aiming the skateboard at the gap between the dumpsters.

"He should sit on the board!" one of Bash's friends exclaimed. To Jake's dismay, Dean and Zachary eagerly agreed.

Jake shot a look of disapproval at his friends.

Zachary ran over to him.

"Dude, if you go through the garbage dumpsters sitting on the board, these guys will think you're awesome, consequently making us awesome too. You gotta do it!" he whispered.

Jake begrudgingly sat down on the skateboard, and after a couple of minutes of assessing the situation, he rolled himself down the slope and silently prayed that he would slip between the dumpsters. Instead, he crashed directly into one of them, which flipped over and spilled garbage all over the driveway—not to mention all over Jake, who was lying on the hard ground listening to everyone laugh hysterically.

It did not take long for a teacher and some parents to show up and start yelling at Jake as if he had orchestrated the entire thing.

***

The next day at school, Jake was practically quivering with fear as he wondered what possible nicknames the popular kids were going to give him after the antics he had reluctantly taken part in at the youth center.

Jake and everyone playing GDSF had been banned from ever going back to the youth center.

"Dude, whatever they call you, just remember that you are a pioneer for riding that skateboard down the slope into that dumpster," Zachary said as he rested his hand on Jake's shoulder.

"I didn't even want to play that stupid game, and now I'm probably going to get a beating or a new nickname," grumbled Jake.

"If it's any consolation, I did manage to get Ms. Thomas to confess that she dated a lot before becoming a teacher…" Zachary said hopefully.

Jake finished his lunch and stood up to return his tray when he noticed Bash and his friends approaching.

Jake considered running away, but he knew that would only make matters worse.

"Jake!" Bash called out.

"Yeah?" he replied.

"That's your name, right?" Bash said with a swagger.

"Yes..." Jake responded, relishing the last few moments he had before surely received a new, less-favorable name.

"You're a genius," Bash said.

"What?" sputtered Jake.

"You got me and the guys kicked out of the youth center with your GDSF idea. We hated going to that place. Nice work," congratulated Bash.

"Thanks," Jake replied.

"Since you're probably not allowed to go back, maybe we can hang out next weekend. Cool?" said Bash.

"Cool," Jake responded as Bash and his goons walked away.

Jake put his tray down and returned to sit with Zachary and Dean. He explained what had happened.

"See, I told you it would be fine!" Zachary exclaimed.

Jake sighed with relief. "I don't think I'll hang out with them, though."

"What? Why not?" Dean inquired incredulously.

"If that's what they like doing, getting kicked out of fun places and seeing things get trashed—literally—then I think I'm better off just hanging out with you guys," Jake responded as he smiled at Zachary and Dean.

"Can we hang out with Bash and his gang?" Zachary asked. "After all, we're the ones who created GDSF…"

Jake scoffed, then smiled.

THE ESCAPE

Jimmi was furious that at the last minute, his mother had canceled her plans to drive him over to his best friend's house. Jimmi was supposed to go hang out at Sam's house on Saturday night, and his mother had agreed to drive him. However, at the last minute, Jimmi's mother remembered that she had an online yoga class that she didn't want to miss.

"It's not fair!" Jimmi vehemently protested. "You said you would drive me. Why did you forget about your class?"

"I didn't plan on forgetting, Jim. Just reschedule it for next weekend," she said calmly.

The more Jimmi tried to reason with his mother, the more furious he got. He wasn't making any progress, and it was becoming increasingly evident that he would not be seeing his friend Sam.

"Fine, have it your way. I tried to reason with you!" Jimmi yelled as he ran to his room and began packing his things.

Jimmi had always wondered where he would go if he ever decided to leave home. Although he had never managed to come up with an answer, he decided that he was about to find out.

Jimmi packed a banana, a water bottle, a map, and some clean underwear into his backpack before putting his wallet in his jeans pocket and opening his bedroom window.

It was late, but there was still light outside. Jimmi climbed out his bedroom window just so his mother would not find out until later that he was gone. He scrambled over the wooden fence around his home and began walking toward the bus station.

Once he got to the bus station, he waited for the bus that dropped him off at school, as he planned to ride it to the end of the route.

Although he had only been gone for a few minutes, he was already thinking about how his mother would react once she found out he was gone.

The bus finally arrived, and Jimmi jumped on. Things inside the bus were completely different on the weekend. On school mornings, he would always sit with other classmates and things on the bus were very quiet and subdued. However, the scene that was unfolding before him now was very different. The bus was packed with loud, obnoxious people much older than he was. Everyone looked at Jimmi as if he was in the wrong place.

Jimmi sat by himself against the window and looked outside, wondering if he had made the right decision. As time passed, more people crammed into the bus until an older man who appeared to be speaking to himself sat by Jimmi. The first thing Jimmi noticed was the bad smell emanating from the stranger next to him.

As the bus approached his usual stop, Jimmi decided the best thing to do would be to get off, which he did.

Once outside, Jimmi relaxed and, for the first time in his life, felt content to be standing so close to his school. He looked at the closed gate and realized he had no idea where to go. Before he could decide where to go next, Jimi suddenly remembered his backpack, which he was no longer holding on to.

Jimmi watched the bus leave with his backpack still there, lying next to the smelly old man who was probably helping himself to Jimmi's banana or a fresh pair of underwear.

Jimmi sat down on the grass and again began imagining how his mother would react once she found out he was gone. Surely by now, she had found out. Jimmi had turned his phone off so she could not call him and beg him to come home.

As the minutes passed and Jimmi just sat and watched cars go by, he began to feel guilty about what he was putting his mother through, but not guilty enough to do anything about it. After about twenty minutes, Jimmi decided to walk in the direction the bus went and hopefully find the shopping center, which he knew was close to the school.

Suddenly, Jimmi realized what would be the best revenge. There was a video game store in the shopping center that he loved going to, and there was a specific game that he wanted his parents to buy him. However, every time he asked, they would tell him it was too violent. Jimmi decided to go into the store and buy it himself—something he had been told he could not do.

Before Jimmi could start toward the shopping center, a car stopped right in front of him and rolled down the window. It was his math teacher, Mr. McMillan.

"Hey, Jimmi! What are you doing here?" asked Mr. McMillan.

"Hi, Mr. McMillan. I had just left something at school, but I'm going home now!" replied Jimmi.

"It's late. How are you getting home?" he asked.

"The bus," replied Jimmi.

"At this time, it's not safe. I'll drive you home," offered Mr. McMillan.

Jimmi protested, but eventually accepted his math teacher's offer.

Fifteen minutes later, Jimmi was right back where he had started.

"Say hi to your parents for me!" Mr. McMillan said as he waved and drove off.

There was no way Jimmi would take the bus or walk all the way back to the shopping center, so he just walked circles around the neighborhood until it was completely dark.

Once there was no more light in the sky, Jimmi walked through the door.

"Hey honey, dinner's almost ready. Can you come down?" he heard his mother call.

"What?!" he sputtered to himself.

"Dinner is almost ready. Please come out of your room and have dinner with us," she continued.

Jimmi couldn't believe it. His mother hadn't even noticed he had left.

Jimmi walked into his room and sat down on his bed. The first thing he realized was that he wasn't even mad. He was too exhausted from walking circles around the house to be angry.

After laughing about the whole situation, Jimmi walked down to join his family for dinner.

"Why didn't you answer your phone?" Jimmi's mother asked.

"I had it turned off so I could sleep," he answered.

"That's what I thought. I didn't want to disturb you, but my yoga thing was canceled, so I could've taken you to your friend's place after all..." she shared.

I'm never escaping again, Jimmi thought, still not mad and finding the entire situation funny. At the end of the day, he decided he preferred being home and eating a warm meal than eating a cold banana by his school on a Saturday night.

HALLOWEEN EGGING

"So, what is this guy's name?" Mitchell asked.

"I'm not sure. Philippe or something. He's French, I think..." David replied.

David was strolling through the forest by his house with his best friend Mitchell, as he did most Sundays before going home and preparing for school the next day. It was a particularly cold afternoon, and the sun would be going down very soon, so the friends were making their way back home.

"Have you met him already?" Mitchell inquired.

"Yeah, my mother dragged me to their house. My mom and his mom were friends in school or something, which means I am forced to be his friend too," answered David.

"How is he?" asked Mitchell.

David shrugged and frowned as he kicked a few branches off the leafy path that led him back to his parent's house.

"He's alright; a bit loud and obnoxious..." admitted David.

Mitchell scoffed and ran his fingers through his messy, auburn hair.

"Oh, he's gonna fit right in here then," Mitchell said.

"C'mon. Not everyone is so bad here," answered David.

"The Harleys are…" Mitchell responded passionately.

David smiled in agreement. "Yeah, I guess the Harleys are pretty awful…"

"The Harleys" was the moniker David and Mitchell had assigned to a group of five kids, all slightly older than them, who lived in the same gated community and were always up to no good. These five boys hung out in the country club at night, playing pool or terrorizing little children and adults alike with their rebellious antics.

Everyone in the gated community rode bicycles, since it was the easiest way to get around the neighborhood. These boys were nicknamed the Harleys because their bikes always seemed to be the biggest and most impressive, with bright stickers and shiny paint, making it seem as if this motley crew of boys was riding around on motorcycles.

David and Mitchell had become best friends several years ago for many reasons. One of the things they always agreed on was their dislike of the Harleys. Although none of the five Harleys members had ever done anything to David or Mitchell, none of the slightly older but much more confident boys had ever even said hi to them or acknowledged their presence in all their years of living in the same gated community.

David zipped up his father's oversized, suede jacket as the day began to get colder.

"Is Philipe already at your place with his mom?" asked Mitchell.

"Yeah, I think so. I should probably hurry; I was supposed to be there by now…" David replied. "See you later, Mitch!"

***

"I thought we were only going for a quick walk close to the house?" David asked as he followed Philippe down the road that led to the country club, which would be filled with grown-ups and older kids at this time.

"I'm just meeting up with some guys I met yesterday at the country club. They were there last night playing pool and they invited me to hang out. Maybe you know them?" asked Philippe.

"What are their names?" David asked apprehensively, pinching the inside of his father's jacket.

As Philipe listed the five names David expected but regretted hearing, he began bracing himself for the meeting he was about to have with Harleys.

***

The country club was very different at night. It was a lot louder, and all the food usually served during the day had been replaced by the smell of beer and popcorn.

David had seen the five large and shiny bicycles parked outside the country club and was already feeling overwhelmed.

One of the Harleys greeted Philippe enthusiastically, as if they had been friends for as long as David and Mitchell had been.

Philippe introduced David to the Harleys. Each of the boys was significantly taller than David, but they all waved to him and greeted him in a much more amicable way than David had expected.

"Yeah, we know this kid. He's always hanging out with the little runt. What's your buddy's name, the really short one?" Axl, one of the Harleys, asked David.

"Mitchell?" he answered.

"Yeah, that one. How come you never hang out with us?" Dennis, another Harley member, asked.

Unsure of what to say, David simply shrugged.

"You look like a runt yourself with that jacket. It's three sizes too big for you!" Axl commented.

Before David could respond, Philippe and the rest of the Harleys began playing pool. David had never played pool, so he just watched.

After about half an hour, Philippe told the other kids that he and David had to get back home before their parents started to worry.

"Are we good for tomorrow?" Axl asked.

"Yeah, of course," Philippe replied.

"You wanna join us, little boy?" Dennis asked David.

"You guys going trick-or-treating?" David asked, knowing that the next day was Halloween.

All the other boys laughed.

"Not exactly," Axl started. "We're gonna egg every house in the neighborhood. It's our Halloween tradition. You wanna join?"

David looked up at the older boys, who all had their eyes locked on David awaiting his response.

"Yeah, I'd love to," David replied.

"That's my guy!" Philippe said as he patted David on the back a little too aggressively.

***

"Are you crazy?" Mitchell asked. "You can't go around egging houses. That's a crime!"

"It's not a crime!" David protested.

The two friends were walking home from school. David had told Mitchell there was some exciting news he had to share, but he had to wait to explain until school was over.

"Yes, it is. You'll go to jail..." warned Mitchell.

"You're just jealous that I'm gonna be hanging out with the Harleys, and you won't!" argued David.

"Of course not. I don't want to hang out with them. They're losers, and if you are friends with them, then you're a loser too!" sputtered Mitchell.

"Well, I'd rather be friends with them than be friends with you!" David exclaimed as he sprinted the last couple of blocks home by himself, leaving his best friend behind.

Once David got home, his mother asked him why he was so excited and if he wanted to start getting his costume ready.

"Mom, I have great news!" David exclaimed.

"What is it, honey?" she asked.

"I'm part of the Harleys now!" he announced.

"The what?" she said.

"And I'm going to be egging houses with them tonight. I'm going to do what cool kids do!" David said proudly.

"You're going to do WHAT?!" David's mother demanded.

***

In retrospect, I probably should not have told Mom about the egging, David pondered as he sat in his bedroom by himself. She'd grounded him immediately.

He had been so excited about being part of the Harleys that he hadn't been able to contain his plans.

Desperate to find a way to still participate in the egging ritual, David snuck down into the kitchen and stole as many eggs as he could from the fridge without his mother noticing before running back upstairs to his room.

David sat down on his bed, laid out two dozen eggs on the blue bedsheet, and started devising his plan. If he couldn't go out egging houses, at least he could egg the only house he still had access to and prove to the Harleys that he was worthy of their friendship despite having failed to show up at the country club at the specified time.

They're all probably riding around on their awesome bikes, having fun wondering why I'm not there, David thought, trying not to accidentally crack an egg in frustration

Determined to prove himself and make up for not showing up at the country club, David opened the window of his room and began dropping eggs on his own house. The first two simply rolled down the roof and broke on the pavement in front of the house.

David shot the next few eggs directly downward as violently as he could and smiled as he saw the front porch begin to take a yellowish hue. Luckily, the eggs did not make too much noise as they rolled down so David felt confident that he could continue launching eggs without his parents immediately finding out.

As David tossed the last few eggs, he failed to hear the front door open or see his dad walk out onto the front porch to investigate what the strange sound was.

David yelped as he saw an egg fall directly on his father's head.

Oh no, David thought as he stood, frozen, in front of the window. He considered retreating and shutting the window quietly but then realized it would be tough to convince his parents that it had suddenly started raining eggs, or that a flying chicken had been circling their home from the skies. Therefore, he could only watch helplessly as his father glared at him angrily.

***

The next morning, David was once again cleaning the front porch since his parents had deemed his efforts to rid it of eggshells and stains from the night before unsatisfactory.

Mitchell passed by on his little green bicycle and saw David on his knees, scrubbing the wooden tiles of his front porch as hard as possible.

"What happened here?" he asked curiously.

"Someone egged my house…" David replied, too embarrassed to tell the truth at first.

"No way! They only egged your house, though. No one else's!" Mitchell exclaimed.

"Yup, no other house was egged, apparently…" David grunted as he tried as hard as he could to remove the yellow residue off the floor.

"Do you need some help?" Mitchell asked.

David looked up at his friend and smiled tentatively.

Mitchell parked his bike by the house and helped David continue cleaning up the mess.

After about five minutes, David confessed what had happened to Mitchell. Mitchell laughed so hard that he started rolling around on the floor getting some eggshell fragments on his white T-shirt.

"I'm sorry for what I said…" David said once Mitchell regained his composure.

"Me too," Mitchell replied.

The friends fist-bumped each other and continued cleaning.

"I don't want to be one of the Harleys. I just wanna be who I am," David finally confessed.

"And who is that?" asked Mitchell

"Someone who eggs his own house and father and then cleans it up the next morning…" David replied. Mitchell once again burst out laughing.

CHAPTER 10

FIVE STORIES ABOUT THE SIMPLE THINGS IN LIFE

THE UNDERGROUND SONG

The moment I walked into the small underground apartment, I immediately knew that I would not be staying there that night. There was barely any space for me to put my things and the decor was very bleak. There was a window with a view of a cement wall and the garbage bins. If you got close enough to the window, you could look up and see people's feet passing by.

My girlfriend Carole lived about two hours away by train, but at least it was a big house where I would feel comfortable. Carole normally lived in the city, but was staying at her parents' place for the weekend. I sent her a quick message saying that I would be staying over at her parents' place with her because I hated the apartment I had rented.

Carole was overwhelmed with joy when she heard the news. I quickly got my stuff packed and headed over to the train station. Luckily, it was so late at night that the trip was not as long as I had predicted it to be.

Carole picked me up from the train station and drove me to her parents' home. Once inside, her parents questioned me about what had been so terrible about the apartment.

"It simply isn't what was advertised. I expected something much bigger and more modern," I explained.

As I described the apartment, Carole grew concerned and felt bad for me.

"Tomorrow, I will go sleep there with you if you want," she offered.

I agreed, considering I had only brought clothes to stay the one night at her parents' house.

The next morning, Carole and I spent the day together in her hometown just walking around and visiting the shops. She could tell that I was anxious about going back to stay in the underground apartment, but it was all I could afford at the time.

Once the sun went down, Carole joined me on the train ride back to the city so she could keep me company in the small apartment. On the trip there, Carole kept thinking of ways to make the apartment look nice and feel less depressing.

When we arrived at the place, there was a large group of drunk old men standing by the door. Carole and I both did our best to ignore them as we entered the building.

"Which floor is it?" Carole asked.

"It's underground…" I answered gloomily.

We both made our way down to the basement and I opened the door for Carole. I flinched at the fact that I could still hear the drunk old men yelling above our heads.

Carole could see the worry and discomfort on my face. She surveyed the apartment as if trying to find a hidden corpse.

"Has this place been renovated since last night?" Carole inquired.

"No, why?" I asked.

"Because it's not bad at all…" she commented.

I turned to look at Carole incredulously.

"Not bad? It's so small and you can hear all the cars passing by over our heads, not to mention the drunk people talking!" I retorted.

Upon hearing my response, Carole looked at me in the way only someone who had known me for years could. She was not surprised by my reaction, but it was clear that she felt differently about the place we were standing in.

"I think you are just focusing on the negative," she gently chided.

"That's because there is no positive to speak of, and even if there was, we wouldn't be able to see it because the noise from outside is driving me crazy!" I replied.

Carole smiled and began wandering around the apartment looking for something. Once she found what she was looking for, she walked over to my backpack and removed my small, portable speakers.

"What are you doing?" I asked.

"Fixing your problems," she answered.

"How?" I challenged.

"I'll show you," she replied calmly.

"Unless you pull out a plane ticket out of here, I don't see how I'm gonna feel better," I grumbled.

Despite my frustrated tone, Carole remained calm and confident about what she was doing. She connected the speakers to one of the wall outlets and then began playing music. She scrolled through her phone until she found the right song and then looked up at me with a beaming smile.

As soon as I heard my favorite song start playing, I felt all my worries and trepidations leave my body, as if I'd been transported back to my childhood home. Upon seeing me visibly relax, Carole walked over to me and took both my hands.

"I know it's not a song to dance to, but maybe we can try," she murmured.

Without saying anything, I began slow dancing to a song that I had heard during some of the best moments of my entire life. I closed my eyes and held Carole tightly in my arms. The moment was so pleasant that I completely forgot about the things that had been bothering me up to that point.

"How did you know to do this?" I asked.

"Sometimes all it takes is a small change in perspective. The problem in our minds can often be larger than the problem outside in the real world, so we need something to tear down the walls we create for ourselves," she whispered.

I looked at Carole and knew that she was right.

That night, Carole and I slept peacefully. I enjoyed being in the little underground apartment; it felt like we had our own little cocoon where no one could bother us and where we had the chance to create a lasting memory for the rest of our lives.

Although we are not together anymore, I still carry the lesson she taught me that night in the underground apartment. Whenever things get a bit too stressful or I am feeling like I am losing my way in life, I just sit down and play the song Carole played for me that night. Even though I have heard it more times than I can count, it still manages to transport me back to the night when we slow danced to that song while a few drunk old men conversed above our heads.

The weight of managing an entire company and supporting a large family can sometimes overwhelm me. When it does, and I feel like I need to escape to the place that Carole showed me I can always go to in moments of stress, I close my eyes and play that song. Even all these years later, that song manages to put a smile on my face and make everything around me disappear just for a couple of minutes.

THE DATE

I met Fabienne in a bar in London a couple of months ago. We had been trying to meet up ever since that night, but something always got in the way. However, in a few hours I would finally be going on a date with the beautiful blonde girl I had met on a night I initially hadn't even wanted to go out.

Fabienne worked at Chanel and had a master's degree from one of the most prestigious universities in London. I had just arrived home from the mall, where I had spent most of the money I had made that month on a new and elegant outfit that I felt would impress Fabienne and not turn her off because I was not as wealthy or successful as she was.

As I waited for Fabienne to arrive, I zipped my coat up to my neck to avoid getting too cold, even though I was eager to show off my new shirt.

Fabienne arrived late but was very apologetic about her tardiness.

We went upstairs and sat down in one of the fanciest restaurants I had ever seen in my life, which I tried very hard not to make too apparent.

Throughout dinner, I talked about all my job prospects and how I had been diligently studying the stock market to start making a very high income. I also talked a lot about luxury cars in a way that made it seem like I could afford one. The truth was, I just loved reading car magazines while I sat in the waiting room at the doctor's or dentist's office.

However, Fabienne seemed uninterested in all the things I had to say.

"I like your shirt," she said.

"Oh, thank you. Yeah, I rarely wear it," I said nonchalantly.

Finally glad to see Fabienne smiling, I removed my coat entirely and stood up to show her the shirt from all angles.

Fabienne immediately started laughing when she saw the price tag still attached.

"What?!" I cried as I sat down and stared at the tag in disbelief.

As embarrassing as that moment was, Fabienne found it highly endearing.

"So the truth is you bought that shirt for this date?" Fabienne asked.

"Yes. I'm sorry I lied," I replied dejectedly.

Fabienne smiled and, for the first time, seemed genuinely interested in me.

After that moment, the conversation flowed much more smoothly. Once the date was over and I had walked her home, I asked Fabienne out on a second date.

"I would love to!" she replied, "but on one condition!"

"What is that?" I asked nervously.

"No more trying to impress me with boring stories about the stock market, and you bring that shirt with the security tag still attached!" she said with a laugh.

I smiled. "You've got a deal!"

LOST

Julian had been working harder than ever before. Being an entrepreneur was even more demanding than he had initially thought it would be. However, he knew he would have to do everything he could to succeed. Julian had recently quit his high-paying, senior management job at a bank so he could pursue his dream of starting his own business.

After a string of sleepless nights and many back-to-back meetings, Julian wondered if this was too much for him and if he should just ask for his old job back.

One Monday morning, Julian sat in front of his computer and began printing some documents that he urgently needed to sign that day. Due to exhaustion, Julian fell asleep with his head on the laptop's keyboard and didn't wake up until an hour later.

When he woke up, Julian realized not only had he missed a call he was supposed to take, but his documents had not been printed because his printer was out of paper.

Julian shot up from his chair, almost knocking his laptop over, and ran out of the house to find the nearest office supply store. He knew there was one a few blocks away, but he was so exhausted that he couldn't remember how to get there.

Julian wandered through the streets of his neighborhood for so long that all sense of urgency and stress eventually subsided. Finally, Julian remembered where the office supply store was.

After getting his documents printed, Julian walked back home, sat down at his laptop, and contemplated what had just happened. Even though he still had a mountain of work to do, he somehow felt a lot more relaxed than he'd been a few hours ago.

Julian grabbed a sheet of white paper from the sheaf he had just purchased and wrote:

Go on walks.

Julian then grabbed some scissors, cut out that sentence, and taped it on his laptop so he would never forget how getting lost taught him one of the best things he could do to clear his head even in the most stressful situations.

To this day, even as busy as Julian is running a highly successful company, he never forgets to go on walks early in the morning and late in the evening to clear his head and make him as productive as possible.

OUT OF PLACE

It had been a while since I had hung out with Gustav and the gang. Ever since I had met Emma, I'd stopped partying and living the wild life I used to lead before she entered my world and tethered me down to earth.

With Emma in my life, I had replaced drinking with exercising. Instead of spending money, I spent time with someone who truly made me happy. However, Gustav had been my best friend since high school, and he'd organized a party in London that I felt compelled to attend, considering it had been months since I hung out with him and the guys.

At the club, I saw everything with new eyes. What I used to think was sophisticated and exciting now seemed shallow and vain. Very wealthy people were showcasing their riches, and tall, beautiful women looked at everyone condescendingly.

Gustav talked to me endlessly about all the parties he had lined up for the coming week, but all I could think about was how uncomfortable Emma looked. None of the girls in our group were speaking to her, and all she was doing was waiting for me to finish talking so she wouldn't be bored.

At that moment, I realized what was important to me. I told Gustav that Emma and I had to go outside for a minute to talk, but instead we proceeded to sneak away from the club and head to the nearest burger joint so we could talk uninterruptedly.

It was one of the best nights of my life because it was the night I realized what was truly important to me and what was just superfluous and superficial.

THE SHIRT

Although it had been over ten years since I'd seen Fabienne, I still kept her in a very special place in my heart. Our first and, sadly, last date had been memorable; I'd accidentally shown up on the date with the price tag still on the shirt I had purchased specifically for that night.

Fabienne was still very successful, but luckily now I was too. There was no need to waste my monthly salary on a nice outfit this time.

Fabienne and I were both recently single, and we had reconnected through a mutual friend of ours from many years ago. Not in my wildest dreams would I have imagined that Fabienne and I would finally go on our long-awaited second date so many years later, both of us having just finished a serious and long-term relationship.

I looked at my closet and tried on several elegant shirts but could not decide on the right one. I couldn't believe that even after all these years, I was still nervous about seeing her.

I looked at my watch and realized that it would be me who was going to be late this time, because I could not make up my mind about what shirt to wear.

After another ten minutes of trying to decide on my outfit, I remembered what I had learned from the last time I had been on a date with Fabienne: not to try and impress her and just to allow myself to be the silly person she enjoyed being around.

I rummaged through old boxes of clothes I rarely wore until I found the shirt I had purchased for our first date many years ago. Instead of a price tag on it, now there was a hole from where the tag had been ripped out.

Smiling, I put on the shirt and was pleasantly surprised to discover that it still fit me. This outfit, with the massive hole in the seam, was ultimately the opposite of what I had had in mind to wear to the date, but I knew Fabienne would appreciate the hilarity.

When I arrived just on time for the date and Fabienne saw the shirt with the hole, she immediately laughed and gave me the strongest, most endearing embrace I'd ever felt in my life. I was glad I had remembered my lesson from our last date to appreciate how critical little moments and gestures can be.

BONUS

A STORY ABOUT CHERISHING WHAT YOU HAVE

GREEN EYES

David had met Eleanor while working as a waiter in a small café next to the apartment he lived in with four other people. Eleanor was in culinary school at the time and juggled working as a waitress, her schoolwork, and taking care of her sick mother. However, despite all of her daily responsibilities, she always remained positive and enthusiastic about life.

The hours at the café were long and arduous, but ever since Eleanor had started working, the job felt less demanding and more enjoyable to David. Eleanor had auburn hair and a very fair complexion. Her eyes were a striking shade of green.

One evening, during an impromptu after-work trip to the bar for some drinks with a few people who worked at the café, David mustered up the courage to ask Eleanor out on a date. To his surprise and chagrin, Eleanor seemed reluctant.

"I'm sorry; I hope I didn't make you uncomfortable," David said as he sat next to Eleanor in a leather booth at the bar close to the café where they worked that the staff frequented on Friday nights.

"No, it's not that. You're a great guy, and I would love to go out on a date with you..." said Eleanor hesitantly.

David expected her to keep talking and braced for a rejection that did not come. After a few minutes had passed since Eleanor's seemingly troubled answer, David smiled and arranged for them to go out for dinner the next night.

During dinner, Eleanor confessed that she was having trouble accepting dates because of the bad experience she had had with her previous boyfriend. David decided not to pry and leave the issue alone. Still, Eleanor seemed compelled to explain, perhaps due to a sense of guilt for reacting so unenthusiastically to David's invitation to dinner the night before.

"I was dating this guy who I liked. We were very serious, but one day he just disappeared," shared Eleanor.

"Like, completely?" David asked, feeling somewhat foolish about the nature of his question.

"He wrote to me a month later explaining why he left me in such a devastating way. He said that he felt I was holding him back because I wasn't as successful as he was and that he wanted to find someone with the same aspirations as him…" whispered Eleanor.

"What a jerk!"" David exclaimed.

Eleanor went on to elaborate that ever since that moment, she felt a little nervous about going on dates and that she liked David, so she did not want to ruin their friendship if things did not go well.

David assured her that she had nothing to worry about, and he meant it when he said that he would never do anything as malicious as what her ex-boyfriend had done to her.

"I suppose he felt the grass was greener without me," Eleanor said dejectedly.

"How could anyone want any green that's different from the one in your eyes?" David asked, knowing full well he had just recited a cheesy pickup line that would put the margarita pizza before him to shame. However, Eleanor smiled, which made David smile too.

After a couple more dates and introducing Eleanor to his minuscule apartment and the many people living there at the time, David finally asked Eleanor to be his girlfriend, to which she said yes—this time without any hesitation.

***

David and Eleanor had been dating for almost two years when he received a letter informing him that he had been accepted to attend one of the most prestigious universities in the country on a full scholarship.

After running around his cramped kitchen and accidentally knocking over several unwashed pots and pans, David called Eleanor and almost cried when he told her the news. Eleanor did cry with excitement.

That night, they went to dinner at a particularly fancy restaurant that they had always said they would go to one day when they either had the funds or a special enough reason to dine there.

David put on the one suit he had, which he had worn only once for his high school graduation about four years ago, even though it was now two sizes too small. Eleanor put on a green dress that David loved because it made her green eyes pop.

"Here is to an amazing new future," Eleanor said as she raised a glass to David's new opportunity.

"Which, don't forget, involves the new apartment we will be getting next year! Hopefully we'll find something good!" David added before raising his glass next to Eleanor's.

"Do you still want to do that? I've been meaning to start looking but I haven't been sure if it's the right thing to do yet," she said slowly.

"Of course, I want to. I will help you search and I'm sure we'll find something right for the both of us!" enthused David.

Just like when David had asked Eleanor out on their first date, she seemed hesitant and troubled.

David lowered his glass of champagne back onto the white tablecloth.

"Do you not want to live together anymore? Did something change?" he asked gently.

"Nothing changed for me. Something changed for you, and I'm scared that you're going to surprise me with more changes," she confessed.

David looked at her as if she had just said something very foolish.

"Have I not proven to you that I am not going to leave or run away? Trust me. This is good for both of us, not just me," he promised.

Eleanor smiled—the same gorgeous smile that made David become interested in her in the first place. Eleanor lifted her glass to finish the toast with David, who downed his glass of champagne almost entirely in one swallow.

Eleanor continued to smile, but it was clear that something was still on her mind. However, for the rest of the evening, she did her best to make the night entirely about David and the fantastic future that surely awaited.

***

Although David was only in his fourth month of college, he already seemed like a completely different person. At first, Eleanor loved seeing him so motivated and enthusiastic. However, as time passed, it became increasingly difficult to get in touch with him during the day or to talk about anything other than the new friends David had made and all the things they got up to during the week.

Eleanor was always supportive and was wary about mentioning how she felt David was drifting farther and farther away from her as time passed.

During dinner one night, Eleanor decided to bring up something that had been bothering her in hopes of getting an answer from David that would assuage her worries.

"I found a nice apartment today. I think it would be perfect for us. Have you found anything?" Eleanor said as she put down her glass of wine.

David kept his gaze focused on his food, which made Eleanor think he didn't hear her.

"I've been meaning to talk to you about that," he mumbled.

"What is it?"

"I've been talking to the guys at school. We're thinking of living together on campus next year; that way, we can be close to the student bar and hang out every day. I was going to bring this up earlier, but you know how busy I've been..." he trailed off.

Eleanor did not respond. She felt a knot in her stomach, and it was not because of the food she was eating.

David explained the situation further, but Eleanor struggled to pay attention.

"When would you be moving in with them?" she finally asked.

"We were thinking in a couple of weeks," David said, oblivious to her discomfort.

Rather than air her grievances, Eleanor remained quiet the rest of the evening in the hope that David would notice that she was upset. But he never did. Instead, he continued talking about how he and his friends would form a fine watch collectors society and recruit as many members as possible to meet wealthy people from campus. Eleanor did her best to smile.

***

After about six months, Eleanor stopped hearing from David. They were still together, but he often complained that he was too busy to visit her at her parents' place, where she now lived.

David spent all his time with his friends in the dormitory. One day, during one of the meetings of the fine watch society they'd started, one of the other students began talking about the importance of having the right shade of green on a particular type of watch. The student passed the watch around, and when it got to David, he couldn't take his eyes off it. The shade of green on the watch was exactly the same shade of green as Eleanor's eyes.

Like a man in a dream, David returned the watch and shot up from his chair. David ran up to his room and called Eleanor, who did not answer her phone.

David then called Eleanor's parents' house. Eleanor's mother picked up.

"Mrs. Mayne? It's David. Is Eleanor there?" he asked frantically.

There was a long pause from Eleanor's mother.

"No, she always works at this time. She has been for several months now..." she finally said.

"Work? Where?" David demanded.

After another uncomfortable silence, Eleanor's mother continued. "Eleanor has been working a night shift at the café where you two met. It's about two hours away from here, so we barely ever see her..."

David had no idea Eleanor had gone back to working at the café and was pulling a night shift. What he did know was that her parents' house was two hours away from the café, which meant that she was getting very little sleep.

David hung up the phone and ran to the café where he and Eleanor had met.

There she was, looking tired but still smiling.

David ran up to her and hugged her as hard as he could.

"I'm so sorry; I am so sorry for forgetting you. That will never happen again!" he promised.

Eleanor finally could no longer contain her emotions and started crying too.

A month later, David returned to his job at the café and moved in with Eleanor in the apartment where they were initially supposed to live.

After that strange moment in his dormitory lounge where he saw the same shade of green on a watch as in his girlfriend's eyes, he never forgot to remember that it is not only the simplest of things that can remind you of what is most important in life, but also that the simplest things are usually the most important things.